the
WORD
& You

the WORD & You

United Church Press
Cleveland, Ohio

A Lectionary-based Exploration of the Bible

Volume 1 (From Proper 18, Year B, to Proper 16, Year C)

Edited by Nan Duerling

United Church Press, Cleveland, Ohio 44115

© 1997 by United Church Press

Printed in the United States of America on acid-free paper

02 01 00 99 98 97   5 4 3 2 1

Library of Congress Cataloging-in-Publication Data

The Word and you : a lectionary-based exploration of the Bible /
    edited by Nan Duerling.
            p.   cm.
        Includes index.
        Contents: v. 1, From proper 18, year B, to proper 16, year C.
        ISBN 0-8298-1165-6 (alk. paper)
        1. Bible—Study and teaching. 2. Common lectionary (1992)—Study and
teaching. I. Duerling, Nan.
    BS600.2.W67 1997
    264'.34—DC21   97-16314
                                                          CIP

Contents

An Invitation into the Word

Welcome to an exciting spiritual and biblical journey through the church year with *The Word and You: A Lectionary-based Exploration of the Bible*. This resource, which is organized around readings from the *Revised Common Lectionary*, will help you to explore the Scriptures using a systematic plan that includes the seasons and festivals throughout the Christian calendar. Many Christians have found that the use of the lectionary gives vitality and focus to their corporate worship while strengthening their individual understanding and response to the Bible's claim upon their lives.

The Word and You is a Scripture-centered study designed to deepen and broaden your spiritual life through engagement with the stories and teachings of the Bible. Some art, lyrics, and literature are included in this volume to enrich your experience of God's presence in your life, in your faith community, and in all creation. Your encounter with the Word of God may spark questions, evoke prayer, inspire individual and corporate response, and motivate new or renewed commitments. Our hope is that you will be nurtured and challenged by the written Word so that it may become the living Word that guides your daily journey of faith.

Using *The Word and You*

The Word and You may be used in a variety of settings. Some readers will use it as a guide for independent study. Adult Bible study groups that meet on Sunday morning or during the week may choose it for their text. If you participate in such a group, you will have the benefit of exchanging ideas and insights with other members of the community of faith. Some of these groups may also be using the adult leader's and learner's guides of *The Inviting Word*, a curriculum that encompasses all age levels so that everyone in the congregation is experiencing the same lectionary passage on a particular Sunday.

Since *The Word and You* is based on the lectionary, which is the centerpiece of worship in many congregations, the lesson progresses in much the same way that a worship service does.

- In the upper right-hand corner you will notice the liturgical date to designate the week for which a particular reading is appropriate. These dates correspond to the church calendar as set forth in the *Revised Common Lectionary*, a three-year cycle (Years A, B, and C) of readings used in churches of many denominations as the focus of preaching and worship. The readings generally include a passage from the Hebrew Scriptures (Old Testament), Psalms, Gospels, and Epistles or other New Testament writings. During the lengthy season following Pentecost, which varies in length depending upon when Easter occurs, the lessons are referred to as Propers. The current volume of *The Word and You* runs from Proper 18 of Year B through Proper 16 of Year C. Two subsequent volumes of *The Word and You* will complete the lectionary cycles.

- Under the title, you will find a verse or two of scripture that contains the core of the theme for the week.
- The scripture designated as the "Bible Reading" is the main text of the lesson.
- The "Additional Bible Readings" include the rest of the lectionary readings for the week.
- The "Enter the Word" section includes two bulleted questions, along with suggestions to help you think about the idea of the Bible reading as it relates to your own life. A prayer is offered at the close of this portion.
- "Engage the Word" opens with a question that will encourage you to consider how the original hearers of this text might have understood it centuries ago and the impact that the text could have had on their faith journeys. The passage that follows the question, written by biblical scholar Dr. Paul Hammer, provides you with background that sets the passage in its context and explores its implications for the original audience and for contemporary Christians as well.
- The "Respond to the Word" segment challenges you to take actions and make commitments that enable the text to live through you and possibly through your faith community.
- In the "Go with the Word" portion you will find a prayer, lyrics, poem, other literary excerpt, or art to activate your imagination so that your head and heart will unite in this study of God's Word.

As each new season of the church year begins, you will find an overview of the season's place in the church year, its dominant color, and an art selection that captures its significance. As you begin this study, you may want to read all of the seasonal dividers for Pentecost (the end of Year B), Advent, Christmas, Epiphany, Lent, Easter, and Pentecost (the beginning of Year C) to get a panoramic sweep of the entire Christian year.

However you choose to use this book, we pray that you will be touched by the presence of the living, loving, forgiving God in your life, for in that is the real purpose of any Bible study.

Aaron Douglas, *The Creation*, 1935,
Howard University Gallery of Art,
Permanent Collection, Washington, D.C.
Used by permission.

Pentecost

The days following the festival of Pentecost, when God gave the gift of the Holy Spirit to the church, constitute the longest season of the Christian calendar. Ordinary time, as this period is known, starts the day after Pentecost, which occurs seven weeks after Easter, and stretches up to the beginning of Advent at the end of November.

The Gospel scriptures of ordinary time focus on the teachings and stories of Jesus. Because these teachings point toward the reign of God, they help to define Christian discipleship and plumb the depths of spiritual life. The main liturgical color for this season is aptly green, for it symbolizes growth in Christ.

Aaron Douglas's painting *The Creation* reminds viewers that God lovingly reaches out to form, sustain, and nurture all creation. Seeds push through the soil and grow into hardy plants that fulfill their inherent potential. Christians too are empowered to grow in a relationship with Christ, which in turn prompts meaningful work and witness for God, just as the Beloved One taught. Envision yourself as the human figure in the painting. Consider how you are growing—or perhaps need to grow—in Christ as you approach this season's scriptures.

Be Opened

Jesus took aside in private, away from the crowd, a person who was deaf and had a speech impediment, and putting his fingers into the person's ears, Jesus spat and touched the person's tongue. Then looking up to heaven, Jesus sighed and said, "Ephphatha," that is, "Be opened." And immediately the person's ears were opened, the tongue was released, and the person spoke plainly.

Mark 7:33–36

Bible Reading: Mark 7:24–37

Additional Bible Readings: Isaiah 35:4–7a
Psalm 125 or Psalm 146
Proverbs 22:1–2, 8–9, 22–23
James 2:1–10 (11–13), 14–17

Enter the Word

- What are your attitudes about faith healing?
- If you were the one who met Jesus in this story, what aspects of your body, mind, or spirit would you ask him to make whole?

Read Mark 7:24–30. In this story a woman from Syrophoenicia

approached Jesus and begged him to help her daughter, who was possessed by an unclean spirit. At first Jesus refused because the woman was a Gentile. Consider the kind of motivation and perseverance that she mustered to convince Jesus to heal her child. Imagine how you might have acted had you been this woman.

Now read the story of another life-changing encounter with Jesus, found in Mark 7:31–37. Be alert for similarities between this story and the previous one.

Identify the verbs in this story. Note that throughout most of the account the person who was deaf is a passive receiver of the action performed first by his friends and later by Jesus. The man himself does not act until he has been healed. Then he speaks plainly, zealously proclaiming what Jesus has done. Imagine what you would have said if you were the man. Suppose you had heard his astounding report. Ponder what you would have thought about Jesus.

> *Gracious Healer, open my body, soul, and spirit to your touch so that I might be made whole. Empower me to hear your words and speak the good news in ways that will draw others to seek you. Amen.*

Engage the Word

- Had you been a member of Mark's community, how might Jesus' healing of the Gentile woman's daughter and the deaf man have helped you to experience God's liberating presence?

Mark wrote for a largely Gentile community some forty years after Jesus' death and resurrection. For Mark, God empowered Jesus with the Holy Spirit in his baptism to free people from bondage that afflicted them (demons, illness, oppressive religion, hunger, fear). Yet it was precisely this liberating Jesus who suffered, died, and was raised. Jesus is God's liberating and suffering Messiah.

The reading from Mark is one such liberating story. Mark's community also may have needed to be opened. The community existed at a time shortly after Nero's persecution and about the time that Roman military power destroyed Jerusalem (70 C.E.). Fearing for their lives, they may have retreated into a kind of closed-off, catacomb existence. Mark did not simply want to tell a story about what happened to a person in Jesus' time. He also may have wanted his hearers to see themselves in that person. They too needed to be opened to "hear" and "speak."

In Mark 7:24–30, Jesus wanted to hide from the crowds he attracted. But he could not escape notice by a Syrophoenician woman with whom a male Jew would have no contact. What is so striking is that this woman's words freed Jesus from an exclusive view and opened him to a vision that included Gentiles.

In the second story (Mark 7:31–37), Jesus, now opened himself, could open another. He touched the man. With an agonizing groan ("sigh" is too weak) and liberating word (Jesus' own Aramaic *ephphatha*), Jesus freed the man to hear and speak.

As found often in Mark's Gospel, Jesus ordered those present not to tell. He did not want his ministry misinterpreted as magic. However, from Mark's perspective after Jesus' death and resurrection, the stories of Jesus' deeds could not be told apart from the whole story (see Mark 9:9). Jesus' deeds need to be seen through the lens of the cross and resurrection.

In spite of Jesus' command, the people simply could not be quiet. The story ends with a hymn-like proclamation. God the creator, who made everything "very good" (Genesis 1:31), now "has done everything well" in Jesus. What happened to the man also resonated with the promise of Isaiah some five hundred years earlier (see Isaiah 35:5–6). The praise of the crowd points to the God of Israel, the God of Genesis and Isaiah, and Psalm 146. This God is at work in Jesus to open God's people to hear and to speak.

Part of that openness is to hear and speak to the concerns of other readings for today (see Psalm 146:7; Proverbs 22:9, 22; James 2:5, 15–16). Personal openness leads to hearing the voices of the hurting and speaking plain words of help and hope.

Respond to the Word

- How can you reach out to someone who needs physical, emotional, or spiritual healing this week and proclaim God's love and healing power to that individual?
- In what areas of your life do you need to be opened? What commitment will you make to allow God to do that?

Go with the Word

Open My Eyes, That I May See

*Open my eyes, that I may see
glimpses of truth thou hast for me;
Place in my hands the wonderful key
that shall unclasp and set me free.
Silently now I wait for thee,
ready, my God, thy will to see;
Open my eyes, illumine me, Spirit divine!*

*Open my ears, that I may hear
voices of truth thou sendest clear;
and while the wave notes fall on my ear,
everything false will disappear.
Silently now I wait for thee,
ready, my God, thy will to see;
Open my ears, illumine me, Spirit divine!*

*Open my mouth, and let me bear
gladly the warm truth everywhere;
Open my heart, and let me prepare
love with thy children thus to share.
Silently now I wait for thee,
ready, my God, thy will to see;
Open my heart, illumine me, Spirit divine!*

Clara H. Scott, 1895

Teach and Be Taught

The Sovereign God has given me the tongue of a teacher, that I may know how to sustain the weary with a word. Morning by morning God wakens—wakens my ear to listen as those who are taught. The Sovereign God has opened my ear, and I was not rebellious.

Isaiah 50:4–5a

Bible Reading: Isaiah 50:4–9a

Additional Bible Readings: Proverbs 1:20–33
                                      Psalm 19 or Psalm 116:1–9
                                      James 3:1–2
                                      Mark 8:27–38

Enter the Word

- What images or memories do the words "Teach and Be Taught" bring to mind?
- An old adage claims that the best way to learn something is to teach it. What personal experiences have you had that confirm or deny the truth of this adage?

Anyone who is in the position of guiding another is a teacher. Instructors, counselors, coaches, mentors, parents, and Sunday school leaders are all teachers. Think of the teacher who most influenced you. Reflect on the ways in which this person helped to shape your life. Now read Isaiah 50:4–9a aloud, hearing the words as if they were being spoken by that teacher.

Read Isaiah 50:4–9a once more. This time imagine that you are the one who has been given "the tongue of a teacher." Consider how you use this gift to lead and teach others. Recall instances when your tongue has encouraged and strengthened those who heard you teach. Also remember times when your words did not "sustain the weary" (v. 4) but instead harshly criticized or belittled them. You may want to write your thoughts in a spiritual journal. Open yourself in order to be taught by God so that you may teach others with the wisdom and compassion of Jesus.

> *Gracious God, for the teachers who have helped me to learn and grow, and for the opportunities that I have had to teach others, I give you thanks. Continue to give me the tongue of the teacher and the heart of the disciple that I may learn and teach in the way of Jesus. Amen.*

Engage the Word

- Imagine yourself as one of the Israelites living in exile in Babylon. Weary and discouraged, you learn that God has called and taught a servant who will now teach you. What impact might this servant-teacher have on you?

Isaiah provides the chance to explore the task of a teacher. In the other readings, Mark tells of Jesus' teaching, James speaks of teachers and the tongue, and the two psalms and Proverbs teach without using the word. The focus here is on Isaiah and Mark.

The Isaiah reading is one of four "servant songs" (the others: Isaiah 42:1–9, 49:1–6, 52:13–53:12) found in the second part of Isaiah (chapters 40–55). This part of Isaiah comes from a prophet during the exile in Babylon in the sixth century before Jesus' birth. He and his community have been torn away from their homeland and forced to live in a foreign land.

The writer defines himself as a teacher whose ear God daily wakens and opens to listen—opens to God's teaching. Last week's lesson included an ear-opening reading from Mark and the psalm reading for today speaks of God's "ear" (Psalm 116:2).

In exile, with people far from home, a teacher does not seek simply to dispense information. A teacher wants to "know how to sustain the weary with a word" (v. 4) and to help people run the course in the hard circumstances of life.

In the midst of his captors, Isaiah's teacher courageously faced physical hurt and demeaning insult. Yet God's help saved him from disgrace and shame and God was near to validate his life (vv. 8–9; see Psalm 116:2–9). The teacher speaks in the first person singular. Yet as he contended with his adversaries he said, "Let us stand up together" (v. 8). He did not stand alone.

In Mark's Gospel, Jesus as teacher also had to contend with adversaries. To confess him as the Messiah did not mean the popular notion of a powerful political-military figure, something Peter first expected and Jesus rebuked as satanic. It meant suffering, rejection, death, resurrection (Mark 8:31; note also 9:31, 10:33–34). To follow him meant self-denial and taking up the cross (v. 34), that is, letting Jesus' self-giving purpose be at the center of life.

Ultimately, teaching does not just involve transmitting knowledge. It involves listening and being taught by God. It involves God-given tongues to "sustain the weary with a word." It involves saying to one another, "Let us [with God's help] stand up together" to face and contend with forces that hurt and rob persons of their dignity. It involves following the teacher who said, "Those who want to save their life will lose it, and those who lose their life for my sake, and for the sake of the gospel, will save it" (Mark 8:35).

Respond to the Word

- How does this Bible passage alter your own understanding of what it means to be a teacher and a learner? What changes might occur if the community of faith were to look at education from your new perspective?
- What action will you take to become more involved as both a teacher and learner, especially within your own community of faith?

Go with the Word

Education . . . becomes an act of depositing, in which the students are the depositories and the teacher is the depositor. Instead of communicating, the teacher issues communiqués and makes deposits that the students patiently receive, memorize, and repeat. This is the "banking" concept of education. . . .

Those truly committed to liberation must reject the banking concept . . . adopting instead a concept of humanity as conscious beings. . . . They must abandon the educational goal of deposit-making and replace it with the posing of the problems of humanity. . . .

In "problem-posing" education, people develop their power to perceive critically *the way they exist* in the world *with which* and *in which* they find themselves; they come to see the world not as a static reality, but as a reality in process, in transformation.

Paulo Freire, *Pedagogy of the Oppressed*, trans. Myra Bergman Ramos
(New York: Seabury Press, 1970), 58, 66.

Welcome the Children

Jesus sat down, called the twelve, and said to them, "Whoever wants to be first must be last of all and servant of all." Then Jesus took a little child and put the child among them; and taking the child in his arms, Jesus said to them, "Whoever welcomes one such child in my name welcomes me, and whoever welcomes me welcomes not me but the one who sent me."

Mark 9:35–37

Bible Reading: Mark 9:30–37

Additional Bible Readings: . Proverbs 31:10–31
                                                            or Jeremiah 11:18–20
                                                        Psalm 1 or Psalm 54
                                                        James 3:13–4:3, 7–8a

Enter the Word

- How do you welcome children into your home, church, or neighborhood?
- Recall a time in your childhood when you felt welcomed, ignored, or rejected by the community of faith. How did that experience affect your relationship with God?

Jesus welcomed everyone. The man who was blind, the prostitute, the leper, and the rich ruler were invited into God's domain. So were the fishermen, the tax collectors, and the poor. Jesus spoke with the religious leaders of his day who disputed with him in private, as well as to the crowds who gathered on the hillside or along the shore to hear him. No credentials of any kind were necessary in order to approach Jesus. His loving arms and insightful words drew people to him. Think about how Jesus welcomes you and assures you of God's love.

Read Mark 9:30–37. Note the contrasts in this passage. In verses 30–32, Jesus speaks profound words about his own future. But the Twelve miss the point and argue about their roles in terms of power and greatness (vv. 33–35). Jesus' welcome of a child in verses 36–37 turns upside down their mistaken understanding of discipleship.

As you reflect on the people in this story, try to identify yourself with each one. Perhaps, like the disciples, you at times are concerned with your own status and "greatness" within the community of faith. Maybe you feel more like the child who is easily ignored by others. Possibly you, like Jesus, embody such compassion that you are willing to go out of your way—even suffer—for the sake of others. Explore how you might be able to be more compassionate, more welcoming of others, and less concerned with your own standing.

Now turn your attention to the readings from Proverbs 31:10–31, Jeremiah 11:18–20, Psalm 1, Psalm 54, and James 3:13–4:3, 7–8a. Examine them to see how they can help you be more open and compassionate toward the powerless.

> *Enable me to welcome all your children in Jesus' name,*
> *as you have welcomed me, so that they may feel loved,*
> *valued, and protected. Amen.*

Engage the Word

- Had you lived in a society that did not hold children in high regard, how might you have responded to Jesus when he said that welcoming and serving a child was the same as welcoming Jesus and the one who sent him?

In a world where every day tens of thousands of children suffer hunger, abuse, and death, Jesus' challenge to welcome and serve children strikes home. Jesus, as well as Mark and his community some forty years later, lived in cultural settings that often devalued and shunted children aside. Jesus' own disciples did this, but Jesus did not (see Mark 10:13–16).

In the context of his disciples' dispute in Mark 9:33–35 about who was greatest (note the additional reading from James 3:13–18), Jesus called them to serve *all*. But then he moved specifically to betrayed, "seen but not heard" children. To welcome them is to welcome the betrayed Jesus himself (see v. 31), as well as the one who sent him to serve (Mark 10:45).

In the earlier part of the Bible reading, for the second time in Mark, Jesus pointed to his suffering, death, and resurrection (v. 31; see also 8:31 and 10:32–34). That was to be his greatest service—giving himself completely and without compromise to others with outreaching and inclusive compassion. Such compassion threatened the self-seeking religious and political power. In other readings for Proper 20, Jeremiah, some six hundred years earlier, also knew such antagonism (Jeremiah 11:18–20), as did the psalmist (Psalm 54:1–3).

Mark's own community lived at a time shortly after Nero's persecution of Christians. It was about the time that the Roman military destroyed Jerusalem (70 C.E.). Mark referred directly to "persecution" as a consequence of following Jesus (10:30). Compassion can be costly.

As Mark's community welcomed children "in his name" (that is, in terms of all Jesus stood for), they could count on Jesus and God's presence with them in difficult times.

Jesus challenges his followers to welcome children, to be welcomed by them, and to know the God who welcomes all.

Respond to the Word

- How can you welcome the child within yourself as one who is loved and cared for by God?
- What steps can you take to assure that all children, as well as others who feel disregarded, know that they are welcomed within the household of God?

Go with the Word

Jesus and the Children

According to a rabbinic treatise, the resurrection of the people of Israel will happen when "God embraces them, presses them to his heart and kisses them, thus bringing them into the life of the world to come" (Seder Elijahu Rabba 17). Something like that has happened to the children. . . .

How did the children merit such a reception? Absolutely no condition is made. The children have not yet reached even "the age of the Law," and they therefore have no merit. Nothing is said about their innocence, their childlike confidence or any other such qualities. . . . God's will is to present the children with [God's realm], and against all human calculation this is done in a totally gratuitous way. . . .

This gratuitous love of God, assured to the children in Jesus' prophetic words and action, turns upside down . . . classifications. Children receive a place of preeminence, if human realities are considered from the point of view of God's [dominion].

Hans-Ruedi Weber, *Jesus and the Children: Biblical Resources for Study and Preaching* (Atlanta: John Knox Press, 1979), 19–20.

Deeds of Power

John said to Jesus, "Teacher, we saw someone casting out demons in your name, and we tried to stop it, because the one who did it was not following us." But Jesus said, "Do not stop such a person; for no one who does a deed of power in my name will be able soon afterward to speak evil of me. Whoever is not against us is for us. For truly I tell you, whoever gives you a cup of water to drink because you bear the name of Christ will by no means lose the reward."

Mark 9:38–41

Bible Reading:	Mark 9:38–50
Additional Bible Readings:	Esther 7:1–6, 9–10; 9:20–22
	Psalm 124 or Psalm 19:7–14
	Numbers 11:4–6, 10–16, 24–29
	James 5:13–20

Enter the Word

- What does the phrase "deeds of power" suggest to you?
- In what ways are your own deeds of power a reflection of your Christian discipleship?

As you read Mark 9:38–50, notice how good deeds and discipleship are intertwined. Observe how such deeds may be performed
by people who are not close followers of Jesus.

Reflect on the deeds of power you have performed, witnessed,
and/or learned of through the media. Imagine a conversation
between Jesus and disciples about these good deeds, even if they
were not overtly performed in Jesus' name. Consider the ways in
which the reading informs your definition of "deeds of power."

After you have explored the passage from Mark, read James
5:13–20. List the deeds of power you find there. Recall how you
have personally experienced at least one of these deeds. Also study
the passages from Numbers, Esther, and Psalms.

> *God of grace, open my heart to the needs of a hurting*
> *world. Empower me so that by your strength I may act*
> *on behalf of others in Jesus' name. Amen.*

Engage the Word

- Suppose you belonged to the early church and were aware
  of the rivalry that existed among some members. You heard
  Jesus say that those who are doing deeds of power in his
  name should not be stopped, even if they are not part of
  your church. How would his words have affected your
  understanding about who was "inside" and "outside" the
  community of faith?

The English phrase "deed of power" translates one word in the
original Greek, *dunamis*, from which comes "dynamite." In Mark it
points to Jesus' healing power (see also Mark 5:30; 6:2, 5, 14) or (as
in the reading from Mark for today) to the exorcising power of
someone other than Jesus' own disciples.

Apparently there was envy and rivalry even among Jesus' first
disciples, as well as among other early Christians. The reading from
Mark for last Sunday showed some of that (Mark 9:33–34; note also
10:35–37). Also, the apostle Paul spoke of it (see, for example,
Philippians 1:15–18). Mark wrote a decade or so after Paul wrote
his Philippians letter in the late 50s Mark did not want his community to exhibit such envy and rivalry nor to limit deeds of power
in Christ's name to themselves.

Jesus' words to his first disciples, who wanted to stop someone "not following us," therefore became good words to Mark's community as well. This is an important point. Jesus' words in the Gospels no longer simply addressed his first followers. The Gospel writers reshaped them to address primarily communities forty, fifty, or sixty years after Jesus' death and resurrection.

In the verses that follow, Mark pulled together various words of Jesus that impinged on the life of the Christian community. That life involved simple acts of hospitality toward one another, such as offering "a cup of water to drink" (v. 40). It involved not hindering new Christians (vv. 42–43, "little ones" means this, not simply children). It involved rejecting misuses of the body that would block commitment to God's reign and separate persons from God (vv. 43–48). "Hell" translates *gehenna*, the burning dump outside the city, and pictures such separation. "Salted with fire" points to a purified community. "Salt" itself signifies a community with flavor and zest. "Peace" (with its rich background in the Hebrew *shalom*) indicates health and harmony in all of life's relationships (vv. 49–50).

Among the additional readings for today, James also pointed to aspects of life within the Christian community, especially to the place of prayer: in suffering, in praise, in sickness, in confession of sin, in petition for healing.

In Numbers, Moses wanted a community of persons, inspired by the Spirit, who could be prophets to speak for God (Numbers 11:29). In Esther 9, with deliverance from their enemies, the community turned from sorrow to gladness and sent "gifts of food to one another and presents to the poor" (v. 22). In their worship, Christian communities often make liturgical use of verses from each of the two psalms (Psalm 124:8, Psalm 19:14).

Mark's healing "deeds of power" are part of the many enriching aspects of an inclusive Christian community in which "whoever is not against us is for us" (Mark 9:40).

Respond to the Word

- Remember deeds of power you or your community of faith have done in the last three months. What deeds could you do in the next three months?
- In what ways are you willing to commit yourself to an active discipleship, one that not only listens and prays but acts compassionately?

Go with the Word

Blessed Be These Hands

Blessed be the works of your hands,
O Holy One.
Blessed be these hands that have touched life.
Blessed be these hands that have nurtured creativity.
Blessed be these hands that have held pain.
Blessed be these hands that have embraced with passion.
Blessed be these hands that have tended gardens.
Blessed be these hands that have closed in anger.
Blessed be these hands that have planted new seeds.
Blessed be these hands that have harvested ripe fields.
Blessed be these hands that have cleaned, washed, mopped, scrubbed.
Blessed be these hands that have become knotty with age.
Blessed be these hands that are wrinkled and scarred from doing justice.
Blessed be these hands that have reached out and been received.
Blessed be these hands that hold the promise of the future.
Blessed be the works of your hands,
O Holy One.

Diann Neu, "In Praise of Hands: A Hand Blessing," *WATERwheel* 2, no. 1 (winter 1989). Published by the Women's Alliance for Theology, Ethics and Ritual, 8035 13th Street, Silver Spring MD 20910 (301-589-2590). Used by permission.

The Work of God's Fingers

When I look at your heavens, the work of your fingers,

the moon and the stars that you have established; what

are human beings that you are mindful of them, mortals

that you care for them? Yet you have made them a little

lower than God, and crowned them with glory and honor.

Psalm 8:3–5

Bible Reading:	Psalm 8
Additional Bible Readings:	Job 1:1, 2:1–10
	Genesis 2:18–24
	Psalm 26
	Hebrews 1:1–4, 2:5–12
	Mark 10:2–16

Enter the Word

- How do you experience God's creative power in nature?
- What gifts of creativity has God given you?

Take your Bible outdoors and enjoy Psalm 8. If you cannot go outdoors, then read the Word as you look at any plants that may be growing indoors or as you look out a window into the sky. Let yourself hear the sounds and see the images of the verses of this Hebrew song. It is a psalm worth remembering by number—8—and by its opening: "O Sovereign, how majestic is your name in all the earth!"

To go deeper into the psalm, try paraphrasing it. Take a phrase or thought at a time and say it in your own words. Make it modern and personal. When you come to a key phrase, list several words or thoughts that come to mind for you.

Perhaps you will discover a new image of God or a new title by which God may be named. One such title might be God, the artist. God is, after all, one who loves to create. The Scriptures tell us that God created us in the divine likeness, in the very image of our Artist. That is a breathtaking assertion. Human history and human nature seem to negate that claim, yet there it is. The image of God in us is that illusive something that moves to imagine, to design, to invent, to construct.

Furthermore, God reaches out to build relationships with each of us. God affirms our gifts of creativity and calls us to give them, to express them. We can express them us to ourselves, each other, the world, and God.

Like a potter, God's fingers have shaped the amoeba, the Andromeda galaxy, and all varieties of humankind as well. We are called not only to thank God for our creation and the creation around us but to be creative ourselves.

> *Creator God, we praise you for the work of your fingers.*
> *Inspire us to create designs, images, and relationships that*
> *reflect your just, loving intentions for all creation. Amen.*

Engage the Word

• How does the psalmist help readers envision God as Creator?

What is the work of "God's fingers"? God does not literally have fingers, but the psalmist used this beautifully poetic symbol to depict God's action (v. 3). God does work through human physical fingers. For example, from the reading for Proper 18, Jesus put his fingers into a person's ears and touched the tongue (Mark 7:33; note also Luke 11:20).

Psalm 8 is a magnificent prayer of praise for God's creative work and mindful care. Here the psalmist addressed God personally with the second person "you" throughout the psalm. The praise of God's name (that is, all that God is and stands for) frames the psalm at the beginning and end (vv. 1, 9).

Contrasts in the psalm are quite amazing. Verse 1a declares

God's glory "above the heavens," that is, above and beyond all human understanding. Yet the next verse speaks of "the mouths of babes and infants"—they who customarily are thought of as without wisdom. Through them God works to stand against and silence God's foes (vv. 1–2).

This focus on the witness of infants and children may make one think of part of the reading from Mark. There Jesus said, "Let the little children come to me; do not hinder them; for to such belongs the realm of God" (Mark 10:14). The majestic God of all creation reigns in the openness and trust and simple words of children (note also Luke 10:21).

Then there is the contrast between the work of God's fingers in the universe and God's relationship with people (vv. 3–4). The psalmist must have known an overwhelming, starry night. How could the great Sovereign of the universe think of seemingly insignificant people on planet earth? Yet the psalm declares that God is mindful of and cares for human beings.

Psalm 8 gives great dignity to human beings. God has made them "a little lower than God" (v. 5) and crowned them with glory and honor. Genesis speaks of human beings as made in God's image (Genesis 1:26)—made to reflect God and what God stands for. But if that is true, then the dominion God has given human beings over the nonhuman creation (vv. 6–8; note also Genesis 1:26) does not mean to selfishly exploit, but to care for all creation as God cares for human beings.

We are the work of God's creative and caring fingers. As such, our fingers are to work to reflect God's creative and caring majesty, both as individuals and as a psalm-singing community.

Respond to the Word

- How can you and your community of faith, like the psalmist, bring new expressions of creativity to your worship experiences?
- What one new activity will you try this week to express your God-given creativity?

Go with the Word

Colorful Creator

Colorful Creator, God of mystery,
thank you for the artist teaching us to see
glimpses of the meaning of the commonplace,
visions of the holy in each human face.

Harmony of ages, God of listening ear,
thank you for composers tuning us to hear
echoes of the Gospel in the songs we sing,
sounds of love and longing from the deepest spring.

Author of our journey, God of near and far,
praise for tale and drama telling who we are,
stripping to the essence struggles of our day,
times of change and conflict when we choose our way.

God of truth and beauty, Poet of the Word,
may we be creators by the Spirit stirred,
open to your presence in our joy and strife,
vessels of the holy coursing through our life.

Gracious Justice

Seek good and not evil, that you may live; and so the Sovereign, the God of hosts, will be with you, just as you have said. Hate evil and love good, and establish justice in the gate; it may be that the Sovereign, the God of hosts, will be gracious to the remnant of Joseph.

Amos 5:14–15

Bible Reading:	Amos 5:6–7, 10–15
Additional Bible Readings:	Job 23:1–9, 16–17
	Psalm 22:1–15 or Psalm 90:12–17
	Hebrews 4:12–16
	Mark 10:17–31

Enter the Word

- What does the word "justice" mean to you?
- How has God's gracious justice been made real in your life?

On an index card, write these portions of verses 14 and 15: *"Seek good and not evil. . . . Hate evil and love good, and establish justice in the gate."* Read this admonition several times as if the prophet were speaking directly to you. Relate these words to your own life by naming concrete examples of ways in which you seek good, hate evil, and work to establish justice.

Now read Amos 5:6–7, 10–15 aloud. Try to project the prophet's righteous indignation in your voice. Now switch places

and be the one who is listening to these difficult words. Imagine
how you would have responded.

Next, fold a sheet of paper in half lengthwise. On the left side
list the injustices committed by the people to whom Amos first
spoke. When you have completed the list, think about current
global, national, and local incidents of injustice that are similar to
your biblical list. Write any parallel examples that come to mind on
the right side of your paper. As you reflect, identify with Amos,
who had been called to be a prophet, that is, one who speaks for
God. Try to write your own prophetic words concerning a particular
injustice. Brainstorm ideas that you can act on to "establish justice"
in at least one situation.

Turn your attention to the additional Bible readings. As you
read Job 23:1–9, 16–17, think about how Job, who wants to lay his
case before God, understands justice. Psalm 22:1–15 will encourage
you to think about the graciousness of God. Look at Hebrews
4:12–16 and ponder the gracious justice of God as embodied in
Jesus, who became our high priest.

As you read Mark 10:17–31, look especially at the verbs in
verse 21: go, sell, give, come, and follow. These words outline
important actions for Christian discipleship. Suppose you were to
do what Jesus told the rich man to do. Imagine how your action
might lead you to "seek good" and "establish justice."

> *Gracious God, you have called us to do justice, and to
> love kindness, and to walk humbly with you. Let these
> prophetic words become reality in my life as I seek good
> and work to establish the gracious justice that you will for
> all. Amen.*

Engage the Word

- How did Amos' call for justice reveal injustice within the
  life of the community of faith in the eighth century B.C.E.?

What is justice? Court systems think of it as balancing the
scales—people getting what they deserve. In biblical understanding,
justice is more than that. It is a positive righting of wrongs in social
systems that exploit the poor and needy. It is not a tit-for-tat justice
but a justice that seeks well-being for all persons in society.

Amos was a southerner from Judah who thundered against injustice in the Northern Kingdom of Israel in the eighth century B.C.E.—a time of national prosperity. Although Israel finally ran him out (Amos 7:10–17), the judgment that Amos proclaimed occurred in the Assyrian conquest not long after (722 B.C.E.).

In the reading, Amos still held out hope for life if Israel sought God. If not, God's judgment would fall (see vv. 1–3, 16–20). The form of the verb "seek" (vv. 6, 14) is plural, so it is a call to the political and religious community ("the house of Joseph" with their worship at Bethel). To seek God meant to turn justice no longer into wormwood (a plant that yields bitter-tasting oil) nor to ruin what is right. Without justice, their religious rituals were hateful to God (see vv. 21–24; note also the references to places of worship in vv. 4–5).

Amos catalogued the wrongs: corrupt and untruthful courts ("in the gate"); trampling and taxing the poor to build houses and plant vineyards for the wealthy; afflicting good people; taking bribes; pushing the needy from the court. In such evil times, Amos said it may prove best to "keep silent" (v. 13).

But if Israel wanted to know God's gracious presence, then they had best heed Amos' rousing call to "seek good and not evil, . . . and establish justice in the gate" (vv. 14–15).

Churches today often do much in the way of social service to meet people's personal needs (food, clothing, housing). However, they often do less in the way of social action to tackle unjust systems that partly cause the need for social service. Amos' challenge is to tackle unjust systems—be they political, economic, penal, religious, or whatever—so that God's gracious, healing justice can be known by all.

Respond to the Word

- How can you raise people's awareness of God's justice to include not only the offering of social services to meet immediate needs but also the restructuring of unjust systems that contributed to those needs in the first place?
- What action will you take this week to "establish justice"?

Go with the Word

The Theology of Pathos

Pathos denotes, not an idea of goodness, but a living care; not an immutable example, but an outgoing challenge, a dynamic relation between God and [humanity]; not mere feeling or passive affection, but an act or attitude composed of various spiritual elements; no mere contemplative survey of the world, but a passionate summons. . . .

There is no dichotomy of pathos and ethos. . . . They do not exist side by side, opposing each other; they involve and presuppose each other. It is because God is the source of justice that [God's] pathos is ethical; and it is because God is absolutely personal— devoid of anything impersonal—that this ethos is full of pathos. . . .

God is concerned about the world, and shares in its fate. Indeed, this is the essence of God's moral nature: [God's] willingness to be intimately involved in the history of [humanity].

Abraham J. Heschel, *The Prophets: Part II* (New York: Harper & Row, 1962), 4, 5.

True Greatness

So Jesus called the disciples and said to them, "You know that among the Gentiles those whom they recognize as their rulers lord it over them. But it is not so among you; but whoever wishes to become great among you must be your servant, and whoever wishes to be first among you must be slave of all. For the Human One came not to be served but to serve, and to give up life as a ransom for many."

Mark 10:42–45

Bible Reading:	Mark 10:35–45
Additional Bible Readings:	Job 38:1–7 (34–41) Isaiah 53:4–12 Psalm 104:1–9, 24, 35c or Psalm 91:9–16 Hebrews 5:1–10

Enter the Word

- How does your society define "greatness"?
- What would need to happen in your life in order for you to say that you had achieved true greatness?

Sit quietly and imagine yourself as one of the disciples walking along the road with Jesus toward Jerusalem. Feel the sand under your feet and the sun on your back. You are talking with another disciple when you notice that James and John motion to Jesus to speak. Read this private conversation in Mark 10:35–40.

Another disciple apparently overheard them talking and soon you and the other nine are furious with James and John. Read Mark 10:41–45 to see how Jesus handles this situation.

James and John equated greatness with power, as evidenced by their request to sit on either side of Jesus in glory. Ponder how you define power. Compare your understandings with those of Jesus, who "came not to be served but to serve" (v. 45). Consider the many ways you serve God, your church, others, and yourself. Identify whatever motivates and empowers you to give yourself in service.

Continue your study by reading Isaiah 53:4–12 and Hebrews 5:1–10. Read also about the greatness of God, as expressed in creative power, in Job 38:1–7 (34–41) and Psalm 104:1–9, 24, and 35c. Read about God's greatness as a powerful deliverer in Psalm 91:9–16. Draw connections between these readings and Mark 10:35–45.

> *Help me to reflect your greatness, O God, as it shows forth in your selfless service to all humanity upon the cross. Amen.*

Engage the Word

- How does Mark's way of telling the story highlight the differences between how Jesus understood greatness and the way the disciples and Mark's own community understood it?

The world often measures greatness in terms of wealth or power or prestige. Jesus had none of these in a worldly sense, but he and his self-giving service demonstrated a greatness that has transformed the lives of countless millions.

Some forty years after Jesus' crucifixion, Mark's community, too, may have been struggling with this question of greatness. For Mark to tell the story about James and John was a way to address that issue in his own community.

In the Gospel of Mark, this story comes immediately after Jesus pointed to his suffering and death for the third time (Mark

10:32–34; see 8:31 and 9:31 for the others). In response to Jesus' announcement of his impending death, John and James asked for power. What incredible insensitivity! Jesus had to say to them, "You do not know what you are asking" (v. 38).

Jesus' own ultimate power and glory did not bypass the cross. He drank the cup of suffering and was baptized into the waters of death. Were his followers willing to follow him in this? They responded, "We are able," and Jesus promised that they would experience this. (Acts 12:1–2 reports that James was martyred.) But it is only God, not Jesus, who finally grants positions of power after obedience unto death (note Philippians 2:8–11).

Jesus then went on to contrast tyrannical power over others with following him as servant or slave (vv. 43–44) to all. He, as the Human One, the one to judge and rule God's new world, himself came to serve and give his life for many (an expression that means all). He ransomed or redeemed (in the language of the slave market), paid the price to bring freedom from the many human bondages and for a new life as God's daughters and sons. This is what outreaching, self-giving service can do (note Hebrews 5:8–9).

Early Christians had to deal with the scandal, the offense, of the cross. Given the popular understanding of the Messiah as a figure of political and military power, a crucified Messiah was a contradiction. But they found in their Scriptures one of the servant songs of Isaiah (Isaiah 52:13–53:12) that could support an understanding of a suffering Messiah. The portrait of a suffering servant that was spoken of five hundred years earlier in Israel's Babylonian exile would now apply to Jesus. The God who worked through a suffering servant to free Israel was the same God who was at work in Jesus as God's liberating Messiah for all.

Jesus' witness proclaims that the mark of true greatness is to serve and to free people for new life.

Respond to the Word

- How can you help others to redefine greatness in terms of loving service?
- If you were to take seriously the idea that true greatness shows forth in service, what would you do this week?

Go with the Word

Prayer for All

God, make us instruments of your peace.
Where there is hatred, let us sow love,
where there is injury, pardon.
where there is doubt, faith.
where there is despair, hope.
where there is sadness, joy.

O Divine Maker,
Grant that we may not so much seek
to be consoled as to console,
to be understood as to understand,
to be loved as to love.

For it is in giving that we receive,
it is in pardoning that we are pardoned,
it is in dying that we are born again
to eternal life.

Francesco Bernardone (St. Francis of Assisi)

A G r e a t C o m p a n y

See, I am going to bring them from the land of the north, and gather them from the farthest parts of the earth, among them those who are blind and lame, those with child and in labor, together; a great company, they shall return here. With weeping they shall come, and with consolations I will lead them back.

Jeremiah 31:8–9a

Bible Reading: Jeremiah 31:7–9

Additional Bible Readings: Job 42:1–6, 10–17
Psalm 34:1–8 (19–22)
  or Psalm 126
Hebrews 7:23–28
Mark 10:46–52

Enter the Word

- When television cameras focus on a large, diverse crowd of people, what do you tend to notice about individuals?
- What emotions have you experienced when returning home after an extended absence?

Settle yourself in a comfortable place. Let your mind drift to times when you were away from home. Maybe you were a young adult moving into barracks or a college dorm, trying to acclimate yourself to a different routine and unknown expectations. Possibly you were forced to leave your home because of a natural disaster, war, or civil unrest. Recall how you felt when you were able to return home. Remember how you were received by those who missed you. Perhaps that homecoming included the whole family for a holiday celebration or other event.

With these remembrances of "exile" and homecoming in mind, read Jeremiah 31:7–9. Imagine yourself being called by God to return home, to gather together with your own people. The prophet proclaims that when God's people return home, no one will be left behind. Everyone will be part of the great company. Try to visualize a large company of people—including yourself—marching on foot toward Jerusalem. Feel the oneness of this diverse, inclusive group. Sense the world around you. Experience the emotions of those who are being restored to their homeland.

Continue your study by reading Job 42:1–6 and 10–17, which speaks of restoration. Also read Psalm 34:1–8 (19–22) and Psalm 126, a prayer for deliverance and restoration of the nation. In Hebrews 7:23–28, Jesus the high priest reconciles and restores sinners unto God. Finally read Mark 10:46–52, the story of Jesus restoring sight to Bartimaeus. Write a reflection in your spiritual journal on God's loving power to restore all persons, regardless of the physical, emotional, or spiritual challenges they face.

> *Merciful God, as I recall those whom you lovingly restored to home and wholeness, help me to see myself and all others as part of that great, inclusive company. Amen.*

Engage the Word

- How would exiles have responded to the news that Jeremiah proclaimed?

A great company is not a mass of people where individuals get lost. It is a gathering of individuals where diversity is honored and no one gets lost.

The prophet Jeremiah himself lived before and during the beginning of Israel's exile in Babylon (586 B.C.E.). Chapters 30–31 appear to have become part of the book of Jeremiah at a later date and hold out hope for return from exile. (To gain a larger context for today's Bible reading, read Jeremiah 31:1–6, 10–14.)

Such hope called for gladness and shouts, proclamation and praise, with a cry, "Save, O God, your people" (v. 7). One reading for today, Psalm 126, has the same spirit: "Our mouth was filled with laughter, and our tongue with shouts of joy" (v. 2).

Jeremiah envisioned a great company of returning people, not only from Babylon. Jews had been scattered in other parts of the Mediterranean and African world as well. That company included all kinds of persons, but the reading reaches out especially to those for whom travel was hard: the blind persons, the lame persons, pregnant women, and women in labor (v. 8). For Jeremiah, that great company was not a crowd. It meant specific persons.

Such homecoming would not be without weeping, but God's comfort would lead them and provide water through the waterless desert and an obstacle-free path. Why would God do this? Because God is the parent of Israel, God's firstborn (v. 9; note Exodus 4:22, Hosea 11:1). Earlier God spoke through the prophet, "I have loved you with an everlasting love; therefore I have continued my faithfulness to you. Again I will build you, and you shall be built" (Jeremiah 31:3–4). God's love builds a great company.

In the reading from Mark (10:46–52), Jesus reached out to a person who was blind. Two stories about persons who were blind frame a section of Mark in which Jesus pointed to his suffering and death three times. In the first story (Mark 8:22–26) Jesus healed the person and instructed him to tell no one.

But in the reading for today, you may see where Jesus' path is taking him (to the cross) and where the healed person follows Jesus "on the way" (v. 52). The healed person too became part of the great company who have experienced God's healing mercy and been given a new path. It is a path that moves finally through tears and weeping to laughter and joy (Psalm 126:2).

Respond to the Word

- What steps can you and/or your community of faith take to help those for whom life's journey is difficult?
- Can you envision the great company that God leads as being completely inclusive? If not, pray that God will open you to include those whom you would leave behind.

Go with the Word

Out of Exile: An Affirmation

We are ministers of a new covenant:
We are coming out of exile!
We are afflicted, but not crushed:
We are coming out of exile!
We are puzzled, but we do not despair:
We are coming out of exile!
We are persecuted, but not overcome:
We are coming out of exile!
We are struck down, but not destroyed:
We are coming out of exile!
We bear in our bodies the death of Jesus,
that his life might show forth in us:
We are coming out of exile!

Miriam Therese Winter, *WomanPrayer, WomanSong* (New York: Crossroad, 1987), 160. © Medical Mission Sisters. Used by permission of the Crossroad Publishing Company.

All Your Heart, All Your Soul, All Your Mind!

One of the scribes came near and heard them disputing with one another, and seeing that Jesus answered them well, the scribe asked Jesus, "Which commandment is the first of all?" Jesus answered, "The first is, 'Hear, O Israel: God is one; you shall love your God with all your heart, and with all your soul, and with all your mind, and with all your strength.' The second is this, 'You shall love your neighbor as yourself.' There is no other commandment greater than these."

Mark 12:28–31

Bible Reading:	Mark 12:28–34
Additional Bible Readings:	Ruth 1:1–18 or Deuteronomy 6:1–9
	Psalm 146 or Psalm 119:1–8
	Hebrews 9:11–14

Enter the Word

- What is your first response when someone issues a command?
- In what ways do you show your love for God, for your neighbor, and for yourself?

34

Read Mark 12:28–34 as if you are encountering it for the first time. Focus on the call to love God "with all your heart, and with all your soul, and with all your mind, and with all your strength" (v. 30). Consider what it means for you to love God in *each* of these ways. Also think of ways in which you can love God in *all* of these ways.

Now reread this passage as if you are one of the religious leaders who hears the scribe ask Jesus, "Which commandment is first of all?" (v. 28). You had hoped Jesus would trip over the answer because you want to have him arrested (v. 12). Instead he responds with sacred words from Deuteronomy 6:4 ("Hear, O Israel") and Leviticus 19:18. Let your facial expression, posture, and muscles express your feelings about Jesus' answer.

Imagine yourself as the scribe to whom Jesus has said, "You are not far from the realm of God" (Mark 12:34). Ponder how Jesus' response has opened new windows of understanding as to what God's commands really mean. Think especially about the role of love in fulfilling commitments.

Continue your Bible study by reading Deuteronomy 6:1–9, one source of Jesus' quote. Be aware of how Psalm 119:1–8 emphasizes the happiness of those who keep God's commandments. Look for concrete examples of love in Ruth 1:1–18. As you read Psalm 146, notice how this hymn of praise shows forth God's love for humanity, a love that is further demonstrated by Jesus' sacrifice on the cross (Hebrews 9:11–14).

> *Help me to be a joyous keeper of your commandments, O God, by loving you with all my heart, soul, mind, and strength and by loving my neighbor as myself. Amen.*

Engage the Word

- How might Mark's community have understood the relationship between Jesus' teaching and the ancient Hebrew Scriptures?

In biblical usage, "love" is not just a warm feeling. It is an active goodwill that responds to God's active goodwill. To love and to like are not the same. Although a person may not like someone, that person is to love even an enemy because that is what God does (see Romans 5:8, 10; Matthew 5:43–48). To love is to seek good for others.

Mark wanted his community to understand that the commandment to love did not start with Jesus. In the context of other disputes (vv. 13–27), a scribe (theological teacher) asked Jesus about the most important commandment. Jesus answered by appealing to two texts about love in Israel's scripture (Deuteronomy 6:4–5 and Leviticus 19:18).

The scribe agreed and affirmed that such love of God and neighbor is more important than all ritual offerings. Temple worship was not an end in itself. Its purpose was to celebrate God's renewing and sacrificial (comprised of two Latin words, it means "holy and whole-making") work and send worshipers out renewed to love in their daily life.

The quotation from Deuteronomy about loving God begins synagogue services for Jews even today. Called the Shema, this reading ties Jews and Christians closely together. It affirms their common loyalty to the one God and calls for love with one's total being: heart (motivating center), soul (life-force), mind (thought), strength (action)—all persons feel and are and think and do. To love God means total commitment to the God who already has loved and who calls for response. Deuteronomy 6:6–9 has a wonderful section on how to keep this love commandment constantly before parents and children.

Love for God is joined with love for neighbor and oneself (Leviticus 19:18). By itself this text might be interpreted narrowly to mean loving only one's own people. But another verse in the same chapter says, "You shall love the alien as yourself, for you were aliens in the land of Egypt" (v. 34). Love knows no boundaries.

Neighbor love is tied to self-love. That double love is rooted in God's love for both. Self-love is not selfish love. It affirms God's love and esteem. For persons to love themselves frees them to love the neighbor whom God also loves.

To show total love for God with every part of one's being and to love neighbor as oneself is to know that God's reign of love is near (v. 34). Jesus lifted up such love and it silenced all his questioners (v. 34).

Respond to the Word

- In what new ways can you fulfill God's command to love?
- For which "neighbor" will you perform a loving action this week? What will you do?

Go with the Word

Christt Be with Me

> I arise today
> Through God's strength to pilot me;
> God's might to uphold me,
> God's wisdom to guide me,
> God's eye to look before me,
> God's ear to hear me,
> God's word to speak for me,
> God's hand to guard me,
> God's way to lie before me,
> God's shield to protect me.
> Christ be with me, Christ before me,
> Christ behind me, Christ in me,
> Christ beneath me, Christ above me,
> Christ on my right, Christ on my left,
> Christ when I lie down, Christ when I sit down,
> Christ when I arise,
> Christ in the heart of every [one] who thinks of me,
> Christ in the mouth of every one who speaks of me,
> Christ in every eye that sees me,
> Christ in every ear that hears me.

St. Patrick (attributed), as reprinted in *Hymns for the Family of God*
(Nashville: Paragon Associates, 1976), no. 643, revised.

Fullness of the Gift

Jesus sat down opposite the treasury, and watched the crowd putting money into the treasury. Many rich people put in large sums. A poor widow came and put in two small copper coins, which are worth a penny. Then Jesus called the disciples and said to them, "Truly I tell you, this poor widow has put in more than all those who are contributing to the treasury. For all of them have contributed out of their abundance; but she out of her poverty has put in everything she had, all she had to live on."

Mark 12:41–44

Bible Reading:	Mark 12:38–44
Additional Bible Readings:	Ruth 3:1–5, 4:13–17 or 1 Kings 17:8–16 Psalm 127 or Psalm 146 Hebrews 9:24–28

Enter the Word

- How do you respond when someone gives you a generous gift?
- What motivates you to give to others?

Prepare to study by sitting quietly and centering yourself. Name the joys and concerns that are on your mind. Listen to hear what God says about them. Feel God's comforting presence.

Read Mark 12:38–44 aloud as if you were reading it to a child. Then write down the basic story, in your own words, without looking back at your Bible. Read over what you have written, referring to the Bible for comparison. Clarify your ideas as necessary. Focus on the details that seem most important. Finally, think about how you would draw the scenes of this story if you were to illustrate it for a children's Bible storybook. You may wish to create these illustrations using a medium of your choice.

Read the story of the widow at Zarephath (1 Kings 17:8–16) using the same approach as for Mark. When you have done so, reflect on the connections, the continuities, and the discontinuities between the two readings.

Finally, divide a sheet of paper into three columns: column one for the widow in the Temple, column two for yourself, and column three for the widow of Zarephath. In the columns for the widows, write features of their stories that seem important to you. In the middle column, write down any connections with your own experiences that come to mind. Examine the intent and fullness of your own offerings to God in light of the offerings of the two widows.

> Generous God, you have given me all that I have. Help me to release my grasp of the time, talents, and financial resources you have entrusted to me so that I may give them back to you as gifts of love that will serve others. In Jesus' name. Amen.

Engage the Word

- How might the story of the widow have been heard by Mark's community, who themselves may have had few financial resources?

Two of the readings for today (Mark 12:38–44 and 1 Kings 17:8–16) tell of the gifts of widows. Another tells of a widow and her widowed mother-in-law (Ruth). A psalm proclaims that God upholds widows (Psalm 146:9). Many biblical writings show such a concern for widows because in the writers' cultural settings women who lost their husbands were usually left without support. In the name of the compassionate God, the writers called their readers to care for such needy persons.

Mark contrasted two kinds of people: some self-seeking scribes (scriptural interpreters) (vv. 38–40) on the one hand with an impoverished widow on the other (vv. 41–44). Mark depicted Jesus as condemning the showy, proud, hypocritical religious leadership of some scribes. Some even took advantage of widows by cheating them out of their houses. Writing forty years after Jesus' ministry, Mark did not want to see such false leadership show itself in his own community.

Within the verses about the widow, Mark contrasted her with the rich (perhaps some religious leaders among them). They put large sums into the Temple treasury. She put in two of the smallest coins. They did it out of their abundance, she out of her poverty— "everything she had, all she had to live on" (v. 44). She was like the widow in the reading from First Kings who gave her last bit of meal and oil to feed the prophet Elijah.

Jesus told his disciples, "Truly I tell you, this poor widow has put in more than all" (v. 43). It was not the quantity but the quality of her giving that counted. The issue was not how much people gave to others, but how much they kept for themselves.

In the story, Jesus watched the people put in their gifts. The poor widow easily could have gone unnoticed. After all, most people would notice big givers. But Jesus noticed her and, from among all who gave, lifted her up as the person of greatest generosity.

Probably many in Mark's community were both poor and persecuted. Financially, they had little to give. The story of the widow must have lifted them and encouraged them in the quality of their commitment. They would give what they had and know Jesus' strong, uplifting affirmation of the fullness of their gift.

Respond to the Word

- In what ways can you encourage the members of your community of faith to be extravagant givers, even if financial resources are limited?
- Which of your time, talents, and treasures will you offer to God this week? How will you make your offering?

Go with the Word

His Widow Complex

. . . [Jesus] was sitting
that morning
in the temple
looking at the treasury-box
in which all kinds of people
were throwing their money
from rattling,
and loud clanking bags.

And then
in that row of rich people
very politely and submissively
greeted by the temple—askaris,
. . . and all the others

. . .

there is again
that widow
with her two five-cent pieces
carefully knotted
in her handkerchief.

She stepped in front of the box
unknotting her coins;
the others were getting impatient
already,
and she dropped her
two five-cent pieces,
and was pushed on
immediately.

Jesus stood up,
and his disciples too,
and he said
to their astonishment:
". . . She gave all she had,
everything;
she gave more than anyone else."

. . .

. . . if our baptism in him
means anything to us,
then our lives too
should integrate
the example
of [the widow]
who gave all [she] had
in view of God. . . .

When he took his bread
that last evening
of his life,
when he took his cup
and said:
"This is my body,
this is my blood,"
he must have been thinking
of . . . that widow
. . . in the temple.

Joseph G. Donders, "His Widow Complex," in *The Jesus Community:
Reflections on the Gospels for the B-Cycle* (Maryknoll, N.Y.: Orbis Books,
1981), 282–84. Used by permission of the author.

God Among Us

God is my chosen portion and cup; you hold my lot. The boundary lines have fallen for me in pleasant places; I have a goodly heritage. I bless God who gives me counsel; in the night also my heart instructs me. I keep God always before me; because God is at my right hand, I shall not be moved.

Psalm 16:5–8

Bible Reading: Psalm 16

Additional Bible Readings: 1 Samuel 1:4–20 or Daniel 12:1–3
                                           1 Samuel 2:1–10
                                           Hebrews 10:11–14 (15–18), 19–25
                                           Mark 13:1–8

Enter the Word

- What signs help you to recognize that God is in our midst?
- How do you experience God's presence, especially in times of trouble?

Read Psalm 16 aloud as a prayer to God. Then reflect on the first phrase of verse 5, "God is my chosen portion and my cup." Consider the ways God supplies your daily physical needs and fills your hungry heart and soul.

Expand your thoughts by using a "free association" exercise.

Take a sheet of paper and write "God among us" at the top.
Halfway down the page, write "God's supportive presence in times
of trouble." Write down words, ideas, and images that come to
mind as you repeat "God among us" to yourself for a minute or two.
Repeat the process with the second phrase.

Possible associations might be Emmanuel, God-with-us in Jesus,
or God's presence in worship. You may relate weight-bearing archi-
tectural beams, or an unexpected surge of inner strength, or the
prayers of others to the idea of God's supportive presence.

Once you have generated a number of thoughts, return to
Psalm 16. As you read the psalm again, find images that reflect the
ones you have listed. In addition, see if any new images emerge.

Turn to the additional Bible readings. Look for ways in which
these passages remind you that God is always present.

> *Gracious God, let your comforting presence undergird me
> in good times and in crises. Enable me to reach out and
> offer a supportive hand to others in your name. Amen.*

Engage the Word

- How might Psalm 16 have helped the Israelites to express
  their faith in God's presence with them and God's ability to
  save them from trouble?

The Psalms reflect the whole range of human experience: from
the depths of despair and death to the heights of thanksgiving and
praise; from the struggle with evil and defeat to the joy of goodness
and victory. They arose over centuries in the life of Israel and finally became a collection of poems and prayers to serve as Israel's
prayer book. As part of the Hebrew Scriptures, they also were part
of the life of Jesus and his followers, so New Testament writers
often refer to the Psalms. Psalm 16 is one of the Psalms that rings
with a very positive experience of God.

The Psalms often combine prayer to God with testimony to
people. In Psalm 16, only verses 1, 5b, 10, and 11 are prayers (they
use the second person "you" to address God). What lies between is
testimony. However, verse 2 quotes a prayer that reflects the spirit
of the entire psalm: "You are my God; I have no good apart from
you."

The psalmist prays for God's protection (v. 1), delights in the "holy ones" (those who trust in the Holy One, v. 3), and will have nothing to do with the practices of those who, to their sorrow, worship other gods (v. 4).

God is the psalmist's good and pleasant destiny (cup, lot) and inheritance ("boundary lines" is surveyor's language) (vv. 5–6). God gives counsel and instruction in the inmost being (v. 7) and is both before and beside the psalmist (v. 8; at trials the defendant is at the "right hand"). As a result, both inner (heart, soul) and outer (body) life are glad and secure (v. 9).

The psalmist concludes with a prayer that affirms God has not given the psalmist up to death (Sheol, Pit) and has shown a life of joy and pleasure forever in the presence and power (right hand) of God (vv. 10–11). Early Christians could relate verses 8–11 to Jesus' resurrection (see Acts 2:25–28).

This is, indeed, an upbeat psalm. So also is Hannah's prayer in response to God's gift of a son (1 Samuel 2:1–10) for whom she had so fervently prayed (1 Samuel 4:1–20). Parts of the Magnificat of Mary (Luke 1:46–55), offered in response to Jesus' coming birth, parallel Hannah's song. Hannah's "heart exults in God" (1 Samuel 2:1) for raising up "the poor from the dust" and "the needy from the ash heap" (v. 8).

The Hebrew word *miktam*, often written beneath the title Psalm 16 in the Bible, suggests that the psalm was inscribed on a wall or stone tablet. This psalm etched in stone, written upon the heart, was a sure promise in the midst of tough times. God was with the psalmist, with Hannah, and with Mary. God is also with us. We can say with the psalmist, "You are my God; I have no good apart from you" (v. 2).

Respond to the Word

- If you were to write a psalm this week, what would you say about God's presence in your life, even in difficult times?
- What specific action can you take to help someone else become aware of God's supportive presence?

Go with the Word

Ground Me in Your Grace

Eternal One,
Silence from whom my words come;
Questioner from whom my questions arise;
Lover of whom all my loves are hints;
Disturber in whom alone I find my rest;
Mystery in whose depths I find healing and myself;
enfold me now in your presence;
restore to me your peace;
renew me through your power;
and ground me in your grace.

I Bring the Truth

Pilate asked Jesus, "So you are a king?" Jesus

answered, "You say that I am a king. For this I was born,

and for this I came into the world, to testify to the truth.

Everyone who belongs to the truth listens to my voice."

Pilate asked Jesus, "What is truth?"

John 18:37–38

Bible Reading: John 18:33–38

Additional Bible Readings: 2 Samuel 23:1–7
                                        or Daniel 7:9–10, 13–14
                                        Psalm 132:1–12 (13–18)
                                        or Psalm 93
                                        Revelation 1:4b–8

Enter the Word

- Have you ever had your word doubted, especially when speaking the truth? How did you feel?
- How do you define "truth"?

Envision yourself in Jesus' place as he was brought before Pilate. Think about how you would have felt in that situation. Read John 18:33–38 aloud as if you were taking the parts of both Jesus and Pilate in their dialogue.

Look carefully at the passage to identify the question that

Pilate keeps repeating and see how Jesus handles it. Probe the way
in which Jesus seems to be putting Pilate on trial.

Much remains unsaid between Pilate and Jesus. If their conversation were to be expanded, imagine what else each might say to
the other. You might find it helpful to write this imaginary dialogue
in your spiritual journal.

Focus on Pilate's final question to Jesus, "What is truth?" Think
of a response to this unanswered question. Consider how Jesus,
often referred to as the Word made Flesh, could just as fittingly be
called the Truth made Flesh.

Turn now to 2 Samuel 23:1–7. As you read, try to make connections between Jesus, the leader who spoke the truth before
Pilate, and King David. Also study the other readings to see how
their words speak the truth to you.

> *Teach me the truth evident in Jesus, O God, so that I*
> *might proclaim it to others. Amen.*

Engage the Word

* How would the account of the trial before Pilate have
  helped John's community know that Jesus expressed God's
  truth?

The Gospel of John was written toward the end of the first century with the purpose of proclaiming Jesus as the Messiah of God
(see John 20:30–31). This message encouraged John's community as
they confronted those who denied Jesus was God's Messiah. Some
of John's community were even excluded from the synagogue for
believing in Christ (see John 9:22, 34; 12:42; 16:2).

John and his community saw Jesus as expressing God's truth.
John's Gospel proclaims Jesus as truth several times prior to the
reading for today. "And the Word became flesh and lived among us
. . . full of grace and truth" (John 1:14). "Jesus said to the Jews who
had believed in him, 'If you continue in my word, you are truly my
disciples; and you will know the truth, and the truth will make you
free' " (John 8:31–32). "Jesus said to [Thomas], 'I am the way, and
the truth, and the life' " (John 14:6).

John 18:33–38 is part of this gospel's account of Jesus on trial before the Roman Pilate. To put this excerpt in context, read John's entire story of the trial (John 18:28–19:16). What is so powerful about the story is that it would appear that Jesus is on trial before Pilate, but really Pilate is on trial before Jesus. Pilate declared Jesus innocent three times (John 18:38; 19:4, 6), but he still delivered Jesus for crucifixion. He feared that he would be in trouble with the Roman emperor were he to let this "King of the Jews" go free.

Yet Pilate knew that this political charge was trumped up to make Jesus appear as a threat to the emperor. Jesus himself clarified this. He proclaimed that his reign was not one more political or military uprising that Rome needed to crush. His reign was not derived from human sources—"from this world" (v. 36). It was a reign that was a gift from God. It was a reign in which Jesus came into this world to testify to the truth; and those on the side of truth would listen to his voice (vv. 36–37; see also John 10:26–27).

But if Jesus' life in general expressed God's truth, what part of it expressed it most deeply? When Pilate asked Jesus, "What is truth?" Jesus gave no verbal response. However, not long after in the story, Jesus is crucified. The cross, God's self-giving love for the world, is the answer. "God so loved the world that God gave God's only Child" (John 3:16). Jesus' reign is the reign of God's love. Truth finally is not words. It is the Word made flesh in Jesus as the Messiah and Child of God.

It is not a truth to crush people but to create peace. It is not a truth of shadows and death but of light and life. It is not a truth of hatred and hurt but of harmony and healing. It is the truth of God's love, lifted up on the cross to draw all people (John 12:32) and to reign over all the world.

Respond to the Word

- What guidelines does your community of faith use for determining truth? Based on your Bible study, how might these guidelines be expanded or altered?
- What action can you take this week to be a bringer of truth to someone who is searching for a deeper relationship with God?

Go with the Word

A Particular Truth

A particular truth can be stated in words—that life is better than death and love than hate, that there is a god or is not, that light travels faster than sound and cancer can sometimes be cured if you discover it in time. But truth itself is another matter, the truth that Pilate asked for, tired and bored and depressed by his long day. Truth itself cannot be stated. Truth simply is, and is what is, the good with the bad, the joy with the despair, the presence and absence of God, the swollen eye, the bird pecking the cobbles for crumbs. Before it is a word, the gospel that is truth is silence, a pregnant silence in its ninth month, and in answer to Pilate's question, Jesus keeps silent, and even with his hands tied behind him manages somehow to hold silence out like a terrible gift.

Frederick Buechner, *Telling the Truth: The Gospel as Tragedy, Comedy and Fairy Tale* (San Francisco: Harper & Row, 1977), 16.

Frans Pourbus the Elder, *Sermon of St. John the Baptist*, Musée des Beaux-Arts, Valenciennes, France (Giraudon/Art Resource, N.Y.). Used by permission.

Advent

During Advent all creation waits expectantly for the coming of Emmanuel, "God with us." Though born in a humble manger, this Chosen One of God is sometimes pictured dressed in purple, the color of royalty. Hence, purple or deep blue is the liturgical color of the four weeks before Christmas.

Advent signals new beginnings, for the Christian year starts on the first Sunday of this season. Advent points back to God's entry into history in the person of Jesus, who lived, died, and was resurrected so that individuals who believe in Jesus might have new life. Advent also points to the future, the long-awaited Second Coming of Christ in grandeur and mystery through which the whole world will be renewed.

Imagine yourself sitting in rapt attention in the crowd depicted in Frans Pourbus the Elder's *Sermon of St. John the Baptist.* Just as John preached the coming of God's Messiah and urged people to prepare for the Messiah's arrival, so too are you to proclaim this good news to others and help them get ready. Advent beckons you to devote time to Scripture study, prayer, meditation, and witness, so that you might be more keenly aware of the amazing possibilities of new life, justice, and peace that Jesus offers to all creation.

Behold the Signs

Jesus said, "There will be signs in the sun, the moon, and the stars, and on the earth distress among nations confused by the roaring of the sea and the waves. People will faint from fear and foreboding of what is coming upon the world, for the powers of the heavens will be shaken."

Luke 21:25–26

Bible Reading: Luke 21:25–36

Additional Bible Readings: Jeremiah 33:14–16
Psalm 25:1–10
1 Thessalonians 3:9–13

Enter the Word

- What are some signs that you routinely encounter?
- How does an understanding of these signs help you to be prepared for what is to come?

Open your study by taking the newspaper and reading several headlines in the international and national news sections. Then pick out one headline that particularly disturbs you and read that entire article. Try to identify the reason(s) that this article troubles you. Possibly you interpret events recounted in the article as a sign of the *eschaton*—the end times—God's judging and fulfilling of human history.

Now place your Bible on top of the newspaper story and read Luke 21:25–36. Reread verses 34–36 and list "the worries of this life" that may prevent you from looking up and around you for the signs of God's reign. Verse 36 goes on to warn us to be alert and to pray at all times for the coming of God's reign and realm. As this Advent season begins, think about your own state of readiness to greet both Bethlehem's Babe and the Risen Christ " 'coming in a cloud' with power and great glory" (v. 27).

Finally, read Jeremiah 33:14–16 and 1 Thessalonians 3:9–13, which both relate to the last days. In Psalm 25:1–10, the psalmist speaks of waiting for God. Connect these passages with your own preparation during Advent.

> *As I wait expectantly for you, Most Holy One, help me to discern aright the signs of the times. Amen.*

Engage the Word

- How might Jesus' teachings on signs have helped members of the early church who awaited his return?

This first Sunday in Advent begins the cycle of the lectionary in which readings from Luke will be the primary Gospel readings until next Advent. The author of the two-part work Luke/Acts wrote toward the end of the first century. The story of Jesus and his ministry is recounted in the Gospel According to Luke, while the history of the early church and its mission is told in the Acts of the Apostles. For Luke, Jesus and the church had a message for his largely Gentile community that broke through the barriers of nation and language, gender and race, religion and social class, to bring "good news of great joy for all the people" (Luke 2:10).

Like other early Christians, Luke lived and wrote after Jesus' first "coming to" (Advent) the world and before his final coming. The church's celebration of Advent includes both, and the Bible reading for this first Sunday in Advent proclaims the latter. Thus the church celebrates the Christmas coming of Jesus in the light of his final coming. It celebrates his coming as a child in the light of his coming as the judge and ruler of God's new world (see Daniel 7:13–14).

The first generation of Christians expected Jesus' final coming in their own lifetime, but it did not occur. Luke as a second- or third-generation Christian had to come to grips with the delay of the coming by releasing it from any timetable, but he still proclaimed the coming as an integral part of the Christian message.

In depicting the signs of Jesus' final coming, early Christians (many of whom were Jewish Christians) drew on Jewish apocalyptic ("revealing") writings like parts of Daniel. They linked Christian hopes for the future to Jewish hopes for God's new world of justice and peace, freedom and joy. Those hopes arose in the midst of national and cosmic upheaval that produced "fear and foreboding" (note vv. 25–26). Luke proclaimed the nearness of God's redemption (v. 28, a term linked to Israel's liberation from bondage) and reign (v. 31).

But that nearness is not to be understood simply as a matter of time. God's redemption and reign are near because they are not only a future hope; for Luke, the first coming of Jesus demonstrated that this redemption and reign had already begun. The "good news of great joy for all people" has already happened and is near—liberating compassion and fear-dispelling love have been born. Yes, for Luke there is a future fullness of God's reign that has yet to be fully realized, and Luke called upon his community to be prepared for it by leading moral and prayerful lives (vv. 34–35).

The way to be ready for the future coming of the Christ is to live the liberating vision of that future that Jesus already embodied and proclaimed. This is to live toward the future in the light of his past and to view the past in the light of the coming full realization of God's reign. With God's redemption and reign already at work, Luke called his community to meet the signs of national and cosmic upheaval and confusion with courage and confidence in God's future.

Respond to the Word

- What signs of Jesus' coming do you see, hear, or otherwise experience as you worship during Advent?
- What commitment will you make to practice spiritual disciplines, including Bible study, so that you will be more alert and prayerful as you await Jesus' coming?

Go with the Word

An Advent Prayer

Silent Word, Creative Act, Hidden Truth, Revealed Love: we wait for you. To be precise, we are impatient for you to come and set things right. We are insecure with our world, fearful of crime in the streets, and anxious about ourselves. We refuse your guidance, but we often wish you would act according to our plans. We seldom pause to consider that you are waiting for us: waiting for some act of contrition; waiting for us to repent and change; waiting for us to listen and respond with a burning passion to your truth, your justice, and your mercy. Furnish us with humble hearts and willing spirits to receive you as you come to us through all the experiences of our lives. Amen.

Allen P. Happe, in *Touch Holiness: Resources for Worship*, ed. Ruth C. Duck and Maren C. Tirabassi (New York: The Pilgrim Press, 1990), 6. Used by permission.

Prepare the Way

The word of God came to John son of Zechariah in the wilderness. He went into all the region around the Jordan, proclaiming a baptism of repentance for the forgiveness of sins, as it is written in the book of the words of the prophet Isaiah, "The voice of one crying out in the wilderness: 'Prepare the way of the Lord, make the paths of the Lord straight.' "

Luke 3:2b–4

Bible Reading: Luke 3:1–6

Additional Bible Readings: Malachi 3:1–4
Luke 1:68–79
Philippians 1:3–11

Enter the Word

- If you are responsible for an event, what difference does your preparation—or lack of it—make in the outcome?
- What preparations are you making to welcome the Messiah?

Read Luke 3:1–6 aloud expressively. Hear the words of Isaiah's prophecy resounding in your ears. Try to visualize John as he invited people to repent, be baptized, and receive forgiveness for their sins.

Ponder what preparing the way for God must have meant to John. Generations had come and gone without experiencing the

56

Messiah's presence, and now John was chosen to announce Jesus' coming. Experience in your own heart and mind the honor, antici- pation, and trepidation John must have felt as he brought the good news to all who had awaited the Messiah!

Imagine that God is sending you somewhere as a prophet to do something and say something that will help people to prepare to encounter God's love as made manifest in Jesus. Think about and/or write an account of your actions as a prophet.

As you read the additional Bible passages you will note numer- ous linkages among them and the primary reading from Luke. In Malachi 3:1–4 the prophet looks ahead to a messenger who will prepare for God's arrival. Luke 1:68–79, a passage of prophecy often called the Benedictus, records how Zechariah, the father of John, understood his son's role as the one who would help the world pre- pare for God's gift of love in Jesus. In Philippians 1:3–11 Paul speaks of the love of the church at Philippi, a congregation that compassionately supported him even during his imprisonment.

> *You who came as a precious Babe and will come again as the Mighty Judge, prepare my heart to receive you. Amen.*

Engage the Word

- How might John's words of preparation to people awaiting the salvation of "all flesh" have been received by Luke's mostly Gentile audience?

As Luke wrote for his community toward the end of the first century, he had a strong concern for the relationship between the church and the Roman Empire. He wanted to create a climate in the Empire that would be favorable toward the proclamation of the good news in Jesus. He did not want to see the Christian move- ment attacked and destroyed as had occurred in Jerusalem in 70 C.E. Luke wanted the Romans to see that the message of Jesus was no military threat but "good news of great joy for all the people" (Luke 2:10). He wanted Christians to see that this message of love reached out to everyone, including the often-hated Romans.

Therefore, Luke is the one gospel writer who placed his story in a Roman political setting as well as in a Jewish religious setting. He did this in the Bible reading for today (vv. 1–2; note also Luke 1:5,

2:1–2). The messages of John the Baptist and Jesus were not detached from history. They occurred in and confronted the political and religious contexts of their times. Their messages were not only for transforming individual lives but for transforming public life as well.

The Bible reading tells of John the Baptist as a preparer of the way for Jesus. John, "son of Zechariah" (v. 2), points back to Zechariah's song in another of today's readings. There Zechariah prophesied of John, "And you, child, will be called the prophet of the Most High; for you will go before God to prepare God's ways, to give knowledge of salvation to God's people by the forgiveness of their sins" (Luke 1:76–77).

As the word of God came to John in the wilderness, he proclaimed "a baptism of repentance for the forgiveness of sins" (v. 3). Ceremonial washing was a part of John's Jewish heritage. He related his baptism ("dipping in water") to repentance (*metanoia*, "mind change") and forgiveness (*aphesis*, "letting go") of sins—the distortion of the relationship with God and others. To prepare for Jesus' coming, John called for mind change and letting go of these past distortions (note the concern for repentance in vv. 7–14).

With his firm desire to relate the events of John and Jesus to the Hebrew Scriptures, Luke applied to John the words of Isaiah recorded some five hundred years earlier. Here Luke followed the Gospel of Mark, one of his sources (see Mark 1:3). But where Mark quoted only one verse from Isaiah (Isaiah 40:3), Luke extended the quotation to include also Isaiah 40:4–5. He wanted especially to proclaim, "and all flesh shall see the salvation of God" (v. 6). It supported Luke's universal concern for all people.

In the political and religious context of his time, Luke wanted his community to see John as a preparer of the way for Jesus to be God's salvation for all. But John was dead. Now they were the messengers to prepare the way for Jesus' coming.

Respond to the Word

- What are some of the ways you and your congregation help the community at large recognize that Jesus is coming?
- To whom will you proclaim news of Jesus' coming in love?

Go with the Word

In the Wilderness

. . .

The wilderness
he preached in
was his own country.
A wilderness
not coming
from the hands of God,
but a jungle
caused by innumerable
human decisions
that were
   wrong,
   short-sighted,
   and selfish.
Decisions
that had created havoc
in the lives
of the many.
   It was in that
   jungle
   that John preached
   and baptized.

. . .

Let us try
to get that wilderness
and also John's word
nearer home,
so that it can cut us
to the bone.

. . .

It is in that forest,
in that jungle
that the word of God
sounds
through John,
saying that once
justice and integrity
are victorious,
the whole of humankind
will be saved,
that Jesus, the savior,
is going to bring
a total difference.
But indicating also
where we come in and
what we should do:
   straightening the paths
   we are walking now,
   preparing a way for
      the Lord,
   filling the valleys and
      potholes,
   leveling the mountains
      and obstacles in us
   and in the lives
   we live. . . .

Joseph G. Donders, *The Jesus Community: Reflections on the Gospels for the B-Cycle* (Maryknoll, N.Y.: Orbis Books, 1981), 11–16. Used by permission of the author.

R e j o i c e !

Rejoice in the Lord always; again I will say, Rejoice. Let your gentleness be known to everyone. The Lord is near.

Philippians 4:4–5

Bible Reading:	Philippians 4:4–7
Additional Bible Readings:	Zephaniah 3:14–20
	Isaiah 12:2–6
	Luke 3:7–18

Enter the Word

- What are some reasons that people have for rejoicing?
- How do you express great joy?

Paul writes, "the peace of God, which surpasses all understanding, will guard your hearts and your minds in Christ Jesus" (Philippians 4:7). As you begin your study, sit comfortably and reflect on how you experience the peace of God in your own life. This quiet time may sharply contrast with the hectic pace of life that is all too common just before Christmas.

Now read aloud Philippians 4:4–7 as if Paul were speaking to you, a beloved member of the church at Philippi. Reflect on your own reasons for rejoicing—you might even want to list them. Give thanks to God for whatever prompts you to rejoice.

Reread this Bible passage, keeping in mind that Paul was in prison when he wrote these uplifting words. Ponder the reason(s) that Paul's spirits were so joyful under such adverse conditions.

Imagine how you would feel and what you might be able to write if you were in a similar situation. Think of a time when you felt as if you were imprisoned by the circumstances of life. Consider the role that worry played for you during this time. Now think about how things could have changed if you had replaced worry with rejoicing, gentleness, and God's peace. Remember that Paul's ability to rejoice did not come from his surroundings—a damp prison cell. Paul rejoiced in spite of his surroundings.

> *Rejoice, and again I say rejoice because you, Gracious God, have blessed the world with Jesus and Jesus' peace. Amen.*

Engage the Word

* What prompted the Jewish community and the early Christian community to rejoice?

Three of the readings for this week include the theme of rejoicing (Zephaniah 3:14, 17; Isaiah 12:3, 6; Philippians 4:4) and the fourth speaks of proclaiming good news (Luke 3:18). Zephaniah called for rejoicing because "[God] is in your midst"; Isaiah because "great in your midst is the Holy One of Israel"; and Paul because "[God] is near." Luke told of John the Baptist's proclaiming good news because "one who is more powerful than I is coming" (3:16). All of them speak of God's presence or coming presence as a reason for rejoicing or proclaiming good news.

Paul has as intimate a relation with the Philippian congregation as with any other. (If possible, read the entire letter; note also Luke's story of what happened to Paul there in Acts 16:11–40, as well as Paul's own reference in 1 Thessalonians 2:1–2.) The church at Philippi lovingly held Paul in its heart (Philippians 1:7) and concretely showed its concern for him (4:10, 15–18).

This letter from prison contains the words for joy and rejoicing some fifteen times, far more than in any other of Paul's letters. In the original Greek, the word for joy—*chara*—has the same root (*char*) as the word for grace, *charis*. Joy is that deep sense of being related to God's grace, even in prison. That is why Paul could write, "Rejoice *in the Lord*," in God's gift in Jesus.

In calling the Philippians to rejoice, Paul did not call them to something he himself had not already done (see Philippians 1:18, 2:17, 4:10). Paul practiced what he preached. To rejoice is to respond gratefully to what God has done in Jesus Christ.

Paul's call for gentleness (v. 5) is based on the gentleness of Christ (see 2 Corinthians 10:1). The mind of Christ identifies with others in compassion and sympathy (see Philippians 2:1–5).

Given that Paul expected Christ's final coming soon, he wrote, "The Lord is near" (v. 5). But that nearness did not have to do only with time but also with space. Christ is near in the present (note Romans 10:8). The one whose final coming Paul awaited was not absent. His grace and peace always are near.

When Paul wrote about worry (v. 6), his use of the original Greek term elsewhere shows that Paul himself did worry about his work with the churches. He called the Philippians not to worry about things that get in the way of God's compassionate work.

The way not to worry worthlessly is to maintain a life of thankful communication with God (v. 6.), the God who "will fully satisfy every need of yours" (Philippians 4:19; note also 4:13). Elsewhere in the letter Paul prays for the Philippians (1:3–4) and invites their prayers for him (1:9). This leads to God's peace, God's *shalom*, God's wholeness, health, and harmony that surpass all understanding.

God's peace in Christ will embrace and guard human hearts and minds (v. 7), both the thinking and feeling parts of human life. Christ's coming brings God's joy and peace.

Respond to the Word

- How can you and your community of faith share your joy with others in response to God's gift of Jesus, the bringer of peace?
- What changes will you make, with God's help, so as to live more joyously and peacefully?

Go with the Word

First Coming

God did not wait till the world was ready,
till . . . nations were at peace.
God came when the Heavens were unsteady,
and prisoners cried out for release.

God did not wait for the perfect time.
God came when the need was deep and great.
God dined with sinners in all their grime,
turned water into wine. God did not wait

till hearts were pure. In joy God came
to a tarnished world of sin and doubt.
To a world like ours, of anguished shame
God came, and God's Light would not go out.

God came to a world which did not mesh,
to heal its tangles, shield its scorn.
In the mystery of the Word made Flesh
the Maker of the stars was born.

We cannot wait till the world is sane
to raise our songs with joyful voice,
for to share our grief, to touch our pain,
God came with Love: Rejoice! Rejoice!

Madeleine L'Engle, "A First Coming," in *A Cry Like a Bell* (Wheaton, Ill.: Harold Shaw, 1987), 57. Revised by Jann Cather Weaver. Used by permission.

Blessed

In those days Mary set out and went with haste to a Judean town in the hill country, where she entered the house of Zechariah and greeted Elizabeth. When Elizabeth heard Mary's greeting, the child leaped in her womb. And Elizabeth was filled with the Holy Spirit and exclaimed with a loud cry, "Blessed are you among women, and blessed is the fruit of your womb."

Luke 1:39–42

Bible Reading: Luke 1:39–55

Additional Bible Readings: Micah 5:2–5a
Psalm 80:1–7
Hebrews 10:5–10

Enter the Word

- What would it mean to you if someone said you were "blessed"?
- How do you experience God's blessing in your own life?

This week's Bible reading focuses on the Magnificat, the song of praise that Mary sings. Read Luke 1:39–55 to see how Mary perceives herself as blessed. Reread verses 46–55 aloud as your own song of praise for blessings. Lift up thanksgiving for your own blessings in prayer. If you would find it helpful, write your own hymn of praise or use an art medium of your choice to illustrate one or more blessings God has bestowed upon you.

As you reflect on the scripture from Luke, notice that Mary and Elizabeth are sharing their stories and their struggles. They turn to each other for support in the faith journeys. Think of one or more individuals who are traveling companions for you. Recall how these persons have helped you mature in the faith. Give thanks for the blessing of their support and counsel.

Now look at Micah 5:2–5a, which prophesies that the shepherd king who is to come will be born in Bethlehem. Psalm 80:1–7, which is a prayer seeking deliverance from Israel's enemies, is addressed to the Shepherd of Israel, a reference to God. Hebrews 10:5–10 records that Jesus came into the world to do God's will. In these final days of Advent let these scripture passages assure you of God's continuing blessings.

> *You who blessed Mary have blessed me too. For the great gift of Jesus Christ I give you thanks, O God. Amen.*

Engage the Word

The main Bible reading for today is part of Luke's infancy stories (chapters 1–2). They promise and proclaim the births of John the Baptist and Jesus. Unlike Mark (who began his story of Jesus with his baptism), Luke pushed the story back to Jesus' birth. He wanted to proclaim that Jesus was God's Messiah not only in his baptism and ministry, death and resurrection, but also in his birth.

Luke 1:39–55 tells the story of the meeting between the two pregnant women, Elizabeth and Mary. The story in part shows John's subordination to Jesus even before they were born. At Jesus' presence in Mary's womb, John leaped for joy in Elizabeth's womb.

Telling this story helped to address a problem present at the time Luke wrote, near the end of the first century. Some people at that time believed that John the Baptist was the Messiah. Luke told later how John himself met that issue (see Luke 3:15–16). The prenatal story of John reinforces the proclamation that Jesus, not John, is the Messiah.

The infancy stories are full of poetic song. This week's reading from Luke includes songs from both Elizabeth and Mary. Filled with the Holy Spirit and overwhelmed by Mary's presence as "the mother of my Lord" (v. 43), Elizabeth blessed both Mary and the one who was to be "the fruit of your womb" (v. 42). She blessed Mary's belief that the fulfillment of God's promise of the Messiah would occur through her (v. 45; note Luke 1:28–38). To bless is to proclaim God's affirmation.

In the story, Mary responded with the Magnificat (from the first word of Mary's response in its Latin form). It is a song that partly parallels Hannah's song at the birth of Samuel (1 Samuel 2:1–10). Mary magnified God and rejoiced that God's favor and great things could rest on a lowly servant whom all future generations would bless (vv. 47–49). God's mercy, on those who honor God from generation to generation, now had happened for her.

Mary's song is revolutionary. It reverses the world's values. God's mercy scatters the proud and brings down the powerful but lifts up the lowly. God's mercy fills the hungry but sends the rich away empty (vv. 52–53). It is a mercy that has helped Israel throughout all its history, fulfilling the promise to Abraham and his descendants (vv. 54–55). That promise also included Abraham's wife Sarah and the miraculous birth of Isaac (see Genesis 15:1–6, 17:15–21, 18:14–19).

Mary's song reached back into the past, but it also proclaimed God's mercy to her in Jesus' coming in the present. That gift of God through her is to touch all future generations and call forth their blessing (v. 48). It is a gift that intends to turn the world of the proud and powerful and rich upside down in order to make it right side up with God's mercy to the lowly and hungry and poor (note also Luke 4:18–19). Jesus' coming brings joy, even to ones before they are born.

Respond to the Word

- What can you do, perhaps with a group, to share God's blessings with others?
- What response will you make today for the blessings God has given you?

Go with the Word

Visitation

> *Each woman listens.*
> *Each speaks:*
> *Ah! the life within you, within me—*
> *   a new revelation:*
> *   God's saving love*
> *   impregnates the universe*
> *   in woman . . .*
> *   joy . . .*
> *   Magnificat!*
> *   Again today*
> *   women tell their*
> *   stories to each other—*
> *   magnificat!*
> *   Listen sisters, listen brothers,*
> *   A new outpouring.*
> *   This time:*
> *   resurrection!*

Mary Southhard, in *Womenpsalms,* ed. Julia Ahlers, Rosemary
Broughton, and Carl Koch (Winona, Minn.: St. Mary's Press, 1992),
10.

Our Lady of Vladimir, twelfth century,
Dormition Cathedral, Moscow, Russia.

Christmas

The waiting of Advent ends at last on Christmas as the human and divine meet in a tiny babe born in a humble manger. During the twelve days of the Christmas season the church celebrates God's presence with us in the person of Jesus. Joy echoes in the melody of the angelic host: "Glory to God in the highest heaven, and on earth peace among those whom God favors!"

While Christian homes and sanctuaries are usually decorated with multicolored lights, live greens, and red bows, the liturgical color of this season is white, for it symbolizes both purity and divinity. The sinless Beloved One of God is now among humanity.

Hearing the angel's news of great joy, the shepherds rushed to see the Savior, the Messiah, born in the city of David. You too are invited into his presence. Meditate on *Our Lady of Vladimir*. Notice how this icon draws attention to the wondrous Child. As Henri Nouwen notes in *Behold the Beauty of the Lord*, Mary's left hand bids the viewer to "move closer to Jesus and discover in that movement the God to whom we belong." During the Christmas season, consider your response to this gracious invitation.

Glory to God!

And suddenly there was with the angel a multitude of the heavenly host, praising God and saying, "Glory to God in the highest heaven, and on earth peace among those whom God favors!"

Luke 2:13–14

Bible Reading: Luke 2:(1–7) 8–20

Additional Bible Readings: Isaiah 62:6–12
                                      Psalm 97
                                      Titus 3:4–7

Enter the Word

- What are some of the ways that people celebrate God's glorious coming in Jesus?
- What impact has Jesus' birth had on you personally?

Read Luke 2:8–20. Try to visualize the scene. Dressed in work clothes, the shepherds were going about their usual business. They were not expecting God to do anything special. Then imagine how the shepherds reacted—and how you might have reacted had you been with them—to the host of angels coming to them.

Think of the times in your life when you were like those shepherds, moving along from day to day, engrossed in your work. Then an event occurred that caused you to remember God. Just like the shepherds, you might have been overwhelmed by God's presence, which impacted you deeply by pulling you out of your ordinary routine and reminding you of God's glory. Meditate on such an event. Be aware of signs of God's glory this week.

Note in verse 10 that the angels had come to bring good news for *all* the people. Consider the impact that Jesus' coming for all people has upon our world today. Wonder about the implications that this joyous news may have for the social and political order of all the nations.

Read Isaiah 62:6–12, Psalm 97, and Titus 3:4–7. Ponder the meaning of God's salvation as you experience it through Jesus.

> *Glorious God, I celebrate your coming and praise you for the revelation of yourself in Bethlehem's Babe. Amen.*

Engage the Word

- Why might the linking of God's glory with human peace be such good news for Luke's readers?

Luke's story of Jesus' birth occurs in the context of political rulers and political obligations (Luke 2:1–3). For Luke, Jesus' coming was no backwater event, unrelated to political, economic, and social realities. It "was not done in a corner" (Acts 26:26).

In Luke's story, it was a political registration requirement that served to place the birth of Jesus in Bethlehem, David's city and the expected place of the Messiah's coming (see Micah 5:2). Though Jesus was born in the humblest of circumstances—in the feeding place of animals—Luke knew that God intended for his coming to feed the world with "good news of great joy for all people" (v. 10). (Bethlehem means "house of bread.")

In the story, the good news came first to shepherds. In that cultural setting, shepherds were societal outcasts. Pious Jews were forbidden to buy meat or milk from a shepherd. Shepherds often were hirelings who would kill and sell the sheep, pocket the money, and tell the owners that the sheep had been killed by a wild beast or had fallen into a ravine.

The shepherds had reason to be terrified and afraid, but (just as Luke often pointed to Jesus' reaching out to include other outcasts) here the good news reached out to them. They went to Bethlehem, told their story, and returned to their flocks glorifying and praising God. The Savior, Messiah, and Sovereign was for them too.

The response to the birth was not only human and earthly; it was angelic and heavenly. With the heavenly host, the universe sang. The song had two prongs: glory to God and peace on earth. Only giving glory to God can lead to peace on earth.

The idolatrous story of the Tower of Babel (Genesis 11:1–9) was the story of glory to humanity in the highest. It led to babbling confusion and the destruction of human community. The humble story of the manger at Bethlehem proclaimed "glory to God in the highest heaven" (v. 14). This is the way to peace on earth.

The New Revised Standard translation reads, "and on earth peace among those whom [God] favors." "Whom God favors" suggests that God favors some and not others. In the original Greek, that phrase is one word. A better sense of it might be translated, "through God's favor (or goodwill)." Then the entire clause would read, "and on earth peace among people through God's goodwill." God wills peace for all people.

That peace is not simply the absence of war and conflict. It is the presence of *shalom*, of God's wholeness and health in all the relationships of human life—with God, with others, with nature. God wants peace on earth and peace in heaven (see Luke 19:38), but Jesus wept because those on earth did not recognize "the things that make for peace" (Luke 19:41–42).

Luke wrote that Mary heard the shepherds' words and "pondered them in her heart" (v. 19). Her pondering must have led to her giving glory to God. She had done this earlier (Luke 1:46–47). In this she points the path to peace: glory to God!

Respond to the Word

- How will you and your family bear witness to God's glory, especially to those who, like the shepherds, do not expect God to come to them because of their lowly state?
- In what ways will you express appreciation for God's glory, as revealed in Jesus, in the coming week?

Go with the Word

Christmas Poem

When the song of the angels is stilled,
When the star in the sky is gone,
When the magi and the shepherds
        have found their way home,
The work of Christmas begins:
To find the lost and lonely one,
To heal the broken soul with love,
To feed hungry children
        with warmth and good food,
To feel the earth below,
        the sky above!

To free the prisoner from all chains,
To make the powerful care,
To rebuild the nations
        with strength of good will,
To see God's children everywhere!

To bring hope to every task you do,
To dance at a baby's new birth,
To make music in an old person's heart,
And sing to the colors of the earth!

Words and music by Jim Strathdee, in response to a Christmas poem
by Howard Thurman. Copyright © 1969 by Desert Flower Music, P.O.
Box 1476, Carmichael CA 95609. Used by permission.

Jesus, Amazing Child

After three days Mary and Joseph found Jesus in the temple, sitting among the teachers, listening to them and asking them questions. And all who heard him were amazed at his understanding and his answers.

Luke 2:46–47

Bible Reading:	Luke 2:41–52
Additional Bible Readings:	1 Samuel 2:18–20, 26
	Psalm 148
	Colossians 3:12–17

Engage the Word

- How does a child that you know amaze you?
- What questions would you have asked the young Jesus?

Think back to your own childhood or teen years. Try to remember someone from whom you learned spiritual values or important lessons about life. Picture how that person looked, spoke, and related to you. Recall how it felt to be with or learn from this person. Also try to remember some questions that you may have asked, as well as how that mentor may have responded to you.

Now read Luke 2:41–52. Retell this story from several points of view, including that of Jesus, the religious leaders, and Jesus' parents. If you find it helpful, write a diary entry detailing the events of the day from the perspective of one or more of the people involved in the story.

Look at the painting by Duccio on page 77. The artist captures the amazement of the teachers in the Temple with Jesus. Imagine yourself in this scene. Think about how you might have reacted to this youth in your presence. Consider the kinds of questions you might have asked and the responses he might have given.

Now read 1 Samuel 2:18–20 and 26 and compare Samuel's story to Jesus' story in Luke. Notice how caring adults helped them grow toward maturity. Savor the words of Psalm 148. Create your own litany of praise to God for the gift of Jesus. Also read Colossians 3:12–17 and reflect on the image of clothing. Pray about the spiritual "clothing" you need as the new year begins.

> *Great are you, O God, and greatly to be praised, for you are truly amazing. Amen.*

Engage the Word

• How did Luke portray Jesus as moving toward maturity?

In his story of Jesus, one thing Luke wanted to emphasize for his community was Jesus' roots in Israel. Though both Jesus' and the church's ministry also reached out to include Gentiles (a major concern of Luke in Acts; note also Luke 2:32), Luke portrayed Jesus, his parents, and others surrounding them as fully observant Jews.

Jesus was circumcised on his eighth day (Luke 2:21). Mary observed the rite of purification and Jesus was dedicated to God (2:22–24). Luke 2:41–52 records that when Jesus was twelve, he and his parents went to the Temple in Jerusalem to observe Passover and what might be called Jesus' bar mitzvah, his becoming a "son of the Law." With Luke's strong concern to show the outreach of the good news to Jews (as well as Gentiles), no one could fault Jesus or his parents for not being true to their heritage.

Further, the Hebrew Scriptures provided a model of another boy who partly paralleled Jesus, namely, Samuel. His mother Hannah dedicated him to God (1 Samuel 1:27–28) and he too (in another reading for today) "continued to grow both in stature and in favor with God and with the people" (1 Samuel 2:26).

Yet the heart of Luke's story of Jesus at twelve was that the focus and direction of his life were no longer to be given by his parents. Though he remained obedient to them, Jesus became his own person. Now he himself could engage the Temple teachers. Now he not only could ask questions but he also could participate in giving amazing answers. Now the focus of his life was no longer his family's house but the house of his heavenly parent.

Jesus' parents had done well in rearing him in their heritage. That heritage had become a part of his life. But then the time came for his parents, as hard as it was for them to understand, to let go. His heavenly parent had a mission for him. After all, his mother had presented him to God as an infant (Luke 2:22). Now he would begin to fulfill his mission as the chosen Child of God.

Yet it was only the beginning. There are eighteen years between the end of Luke 2 and the beginning of Luke 3 where the story of Jesus' public ministry starts. Perhaps Luke provided the link in the last verse of chapter 2. They were years in which "Jesus increased in wisdom and in years [or stature], and in divine and human favor."

Luke knew that Jesus would bring to his public ministry the maturity of years of growth in mind and body and growth in relationships with both God and other people. He would bring the courage of his convictions and the commitment to be faithful in the face of opposition. He would live out his own Hebrew heritage that stood for liberty and justice, for healing and life, for truth and peace. It all began at twelve when he said, "I must be in my Father's house" (Luke 2:49).

Respond to the Word

- How can you and other adults encourage the spiritual searching of children and youth?
- What is one action you can take today to be about God's business?

Go with the Word

How might Jesus have amazed you had you been one of the learned religious leaders?

Duccio di Buoninsegna, *Maesta: Christ among the Doctors*, detail, 1308–1311, Museo dell'Opera Metropolitana, Siena, Italy (Alinari/Art Resource, N.Y.). Used by permission.

Born of God

The Word was in the world, and the world was made through the Word, yet the world did not know the Word. But to all who received the Word, who believed in the name of the Word, power was given to become children of God.

John 1:10, 12

Bible Reading:	John 1:(1–9) 10–18
Additional Bible Readings:	Jeremiah 31:7–14
	Psalm 147:12–20
	or Wisdom of Solomon 10:15–21
	Ephesians 1:3–14

Enter the Word

- What does the phrase "born of God" mean to you?
- How do you see yourself as one born of God?

If possible, look at some pictures of yourself when you were a young child. Recall how significant adults in your life, perhaps especially your parents, loved and cared for you. Think back to the ways that you responded to them—a warm hug, a spontaneous antic, the creation of an artwork with crayons or finger-paint. Now read John 1:(1–9) 10–18. Envision yourself as a child born of God. Write in your journal or mediate on the similarities between your relationship and response to your human parents and to your heavenly parent.

Also read today's additional scriptures. Jeremiah 31:7–14 speaks about God's children returning home to Israel. Psalm 147:12–20 sings praise for God's power and care. Wisdom of Solomon 10:15–21 reminds the reader that wisdom, working through Moses, led the Israelites out of bondage in Egypt. The final passage from Ephesians 1:3–14 offers thanks for God's blessings and refers to our adoption as God's children (v. 5).

> *Help me to respond to the compassionate love and grace that you, O God My Parent, have showered upon me. Amen.*

Engage the Word

- How can today's reading from the Gospel of John help Christians understand what it means to be "born of God"?

Written toward the end of the first century, this gospel powerfully proclaims that Jesus is indeed God's life-giving Messiah and Child. It does so to meet the challenge of those who said he was not God's Messiah and those who denied that God's grace and truth were in him (note John 1:14).

The Prologue (John 1:1–18) introduces the story of Jesus with hymnic poetry, though prose breaks the poetry in vv. 6–8, 15. The gospel writer wanted to make sure that his readers did not confuse John the Baptist with Jesus, God's Messiah and life-bringing light. Late in the first century some people still confused the two.

Further, there were those at that time who wanted to separate the one they saw as the evil God of creation from the good God of salvation. These Gnostics saw creation as the evil from which human beings needed to be saved by the good God of special religious knowledge (*gnosis*).

But John's Gospel links inseparably the God of creation in the Genesis story with the God of salvation in Jesus. The God at work in the Word of creation to bring light and life also is at work in the same Word that in Jesus "became flesh and lived among us" (v. 14) to bring light and life (vv. 4, 5, 9).

Yet how is that light and life to become real for us in our lives? Though all of us are God's *creatures*, for John's Gospel that does not make us God's *children*. Our positive response as creatures to our Creator's love makes us true children.

For this gospel, children are not the biological product of human blood and flesh and will (v. 13). God's outreaching love meets our creaturely rejection of our Creator (John's Gospel calls this "sin") with a grace and truth that can make us God's children.

It is this grace and truth that calls for our reception—for our entering into (i.e., believing) this gift of a new relationship—and thus for our realizing God's gift of power to become God's children. For us to live life in response to God's love is what it means to be "born of God" and to become God's children.

It is not unlike becoming "children" in our families. Simple biological reproduction and birth do not make us true children. What makes us true children is the relationship that is born when love reaches out and a positive response completes the circle of love.

The story of the meeting between Nicodemus and Jesus in John 3 also uses birth language. Nicodemus speaks of being born again, but Jesus speaks of being "born from above" (v. 3; the Greek *anothen* can be translated either way).

Nicodemus thinks in terms of a human experience; Jesus in terms of God's gift of love. Some people speak of their experience as being "born again," but for John's Gospel all children of God are "born from above," no matter how we may have experienced this outreaching love of God, which occurs in a host of different ways. God's love works in many ways "from above" to meet us where we are and to make us truly God's beloved and responsive children.

In the Jeremiah 31 reading God says, "I have become a parent to Israel, and Ephraim is my firstborn" (v. 9). Why? Because God affirms, "I have loved you with an everlasting love" (v. 3). God's love for us creatures did not begin with Jesus. It has been the heart of God from the beginning, seeking to let us and all people be born as God's true children.

Respond to the Word

- What new act of service could your congregation undertake to show God's love for all persons?
- What will you do today in response to God's love?

Go with the Word

Jesus became flesh
so as to show forth the love
of God among us,
a love which is not merely
an expression of good will,
but the power of an
energy which is the heart,
core, and cohesive
force of the universe. . . .
Christ is the human expression
of God to us, and thus we
must try to understand
what God meant in Christ. . . .
Christ is not simply
the new male person,
but one who shows
all persons how to live.
As a human he shows us
what human self-possession
and self-giving are.
Thereby Christ shows us
the link between
divine and human,
the cosmos and its
conscious inhabitants.

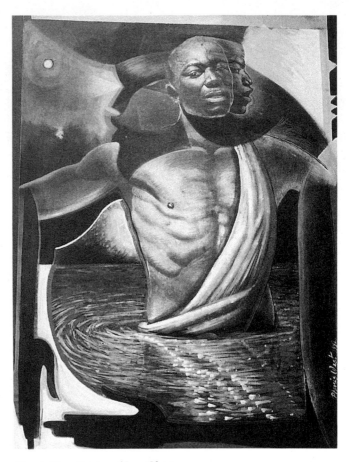

Pheoris West, *Baptism of Jesus Christ*,
artist's collection, Columbus, Ohio.
Used by permission.

Epiphany

Epiphanos—Jesus is shown forth as a light to the nations, the Savior of all. Celebrated on January 6, the twelfth day of Christmas, Epiphany reveals Jesus as the Messiah. The Magi travel from the East to worship this newborn Sovereign. As he is baptized in the Jordan River, the Holy Spirit confirms that Jesus is God's Beloved One. Beginning his public ministry, Jesus turns water into wine at Cana, a sign of the transforming ministry that will unfold over the next three years of his life. The season of Epiphany ends with a crescendo on Transfiguration Sunday, just days before the beginning of Lent, as Jesus is revealed in dazzling splendor upon the mountaintop to three of his disciples and, through the written Word, to all who would follow him.

This liturgical season begins and ends with the celebratory color white. During the remainder of the days, the color is green.

Gaze at the *Baptism of Jesus Christ* by the contemporary North American artist Pheoris West. Note the action depicted in the movement of Jesus' head. Look into Jesus' eyes and imagine what he might be saying about how you have committed yourself to him through your own baptism, just as he committed himself to do the will and work of God. Also consider the depth of commitment that your own congregation has—or could have—when all the members focus single-mindedly on fulfilling their calling as a community of faith.

Jesus Baptized

Now when all the people were baptized, and when Jesus also had been baptized and was praying, the heaven was opened, and the Holy Spirit descended upon him in bodily form like a dove. And a voice came down from heaven, "You are my Child, the Beloved; with you I am well pleased."

Luke 3:21–22

Bible Reading:	Luke 3:15–17, 21–22
Additional Bible Readings:	Isaiah 43:1–7
	Psalm 29
	Acts 8:14–17

Enter the Word

- When people are asked to identify themselves, they answer in a variety of ways: "I'm the principal of Washington High," or "I'm Jennifer's dad," or "I'm a resident of Harbor Center." How do you answer when someone asks you to identify yourself?
- What might be some signs, behaviors, or attitudes that confirm that identity?

Jesus, and the church as well, understood that he was the Beloved Child of God. This identity was confirmed by a voice that came from heaven as he was baptized. Read the account of this event in Luke 3:15–17, 21–22. Imagine John speaking to the crowd (vv. 15–17), the people being baptized (v. 21), Jesus being baptized (v. 21), Jesus praying (v. 21), Jesus receiving the Spirit (v. 22), and Jesus hearing the voice (v. 22).

Reread this passage and picture yourself (1) as a spectator in the crowd, (2) as John, and (3) as Jesus. Meditate on the thoughts, emotions, and sensations you have as you experience the story from these different points of view. If you have been baptized, ponder the meaning of this sacrament in your own life.

> *Loving God, when the waters of the River Jordan washed over Jesus, you identified him as your Beloved Child. Turn my heart toward you as I claim anew the identity that your Word assures me is mine as a beloved child of God. Amen.*

Engage the Word

- How might Jesus' baptism have helped members of the early church figure out their own identity?

When Luke wrote for his congregation toward the end of the first century, some people thought that John the Baptist was the Messiah. Luke reflected this concern in the first verse of today's Bible reading, when John pointed to "one who is more powerful than I" (v. 16). John baptized with water to bring about cleansing and release from past sins. But the one who would come, Jesus the Messiah, would baptize with the Holy Spirit. This Spirit (or *pneuma* in the Greek, which can be translated as "spirit" or "wind" or "breath"; also see Genesis 2:7) would empower people for a new life. That gift of the Spirit also involved purification—turning followers into wheat for the harvest rather than useless chaff (in vv. 16–17, fire can symbolize purification as well as judgment upon evil). John did not understand himself to be the one with such authority to empower and purify (v. 16). He was not the Messiah.

Still, John's preaching and criticism of the political ruler Herod's evil actions landed him in jail (see Mark 6:17–18). In Mark and Matthew's stories of Jesus' baptism, John baptized Jesus. The striking difference in Luke's telling of the story is that John was already in prison when Jesus was baptized (v. 20). Because some people in Luke's time still exalted John, Luke wanted to emphasize that Jesus and his ministry were in no way dependent on John and baptism by him.

Luke wanted to point beyond Jesus' baptism to Jesus' relationship with God. Among the gospel writers, only Luke related Jesus' baptism to prayer (v. 21). Prayer can mean opening oneself to God's will and purpose. It was while Jesus was at prayer that "the heaven was opened" and God's empowering Holy Spirit came upon Jesus. "The bodily form like a dove" points to the Spirit as becoming a real part of Jesus' earthly life.

With the Spirit, God proclaimed Jesus as God's Beloved Child. In the Hebrew Scriptures, Israel sometimes is called God's child in the context of God's liberation of Israel from Egyptian bondage (Exodus 4:22; Hosea 11:1). In today's additional Bible reading from Isaiah, God called Israel by name (Isaiah 43:1). Thus child or "son" pointed to God's liberating action in both Israel and Jesus.

From the original Greek, the traditional words "with you I am well pleased" can be better translated "in you I have willed the good." Jesus is not simply pleasing to God. In the Beloved's baptism and openness in prayer, God proclaimed and empowered Jesus for God's purpose—to be God's liberating agent of "good news of great joy for all people" (Luke 2:10). Luke 4:18–19, a portion of the reading for Epiphany 3, describes that Spirited purpose in even greater detail.

Because Jesus now baptizes with the Holy Spirit, baptism marks us as God's beloved children and agents of God's goodwill in the world today.

Respond to the Word

- How could the world be different if baptized Christians lived out their identity as God's children more faithfully, both as individuals and as the church?
- What ideas does the poem "A Prayer of Confession" give you for specific changes you could make in your life this week?

Go with the Word

A Prayer of Confession
(Based on Isaiah 43)

> God of our lives,
>> you have called us,
>> but we have not listened.
> You have redeemed us,
>> but we do not claim your grace.
> Ignoring our baptism into compassion,
>> we turn from the cries of our sisters and brothers
>> for love and justice, shelter and food.
> Denying our baptism into your realm of truth,
>> we choose to serve other gods.
> Rather than live in faith,
>> we live in fear.
> Open us to your Spirit.
> Give us the strength and will
>> to turn to you.
> Pour out your forgiveness upon us—
>> renew our courage to live out our baptisms.

Jann Cather Weaver, in *The Inviting Word Older Youth Learner's Guide*, Year One (Cleveland, Ohio: United Church Press, 1994), 45. © 1994 by United Church Press. Used by permission.

The Wedding at Cana

When the steward tasted the water that had become wine, and did not know where it came from (though the servants who had drawn the water knew), the steward called the bridegroom and said to him, "Everyone serves the good wine first, and then the inferior wine after the guests have become drunk. But you have kept the good wine until now." Jesus did this, the first of his signs, in Cana of Galilee, and revealed his glory; and the disciples believed in Jesus.

John 2:9–11

Bible Reading:　　　　　　　John 2:1–11

Additional Bible Readings:　　Isaiah 62:1–5
　　　　　　　　　　　　　　　Psalm 36:5–10
　　　　　　　　　　　　　　　1 Corinthians 12:1–11

Enter the Word

- What comes to mind when you think of a wedding?
- What signposts guide your spiritual life?

Visualize yourself at a wedding and the banquet that follows. Enter into the joy of the moment. See the guests as they wait expectantly for the bride and groom to appear. Listen to the words of the one authorized to join them in matrimony. Taste and smell the food of a festive reception.

With these modern images in mind, read John 2:1–11. Pretend that you are one of the disciples. Ask the steward and guests for their opinions about what has happened. Then talk with Mary. Finally, speak with Jesus about what you have witnessed and why that has convinced you to believe in him. Assume it is the next day. Write a letter in your spiritual journal, perhaps addressed to a friend, in which you give details of the day's events.

Review the passage from John, especially verse 11. The most important point of the story is not the miracle itself. Rather, Jesus' turning of water into wine points beyond that action and is a sign that reveals his glory. List some signs that reveal Jesus' glory to you.

Read aloud Isaiah 62:1–5 and Psalm 36:5–10. Look for images in these passages similar to those in John. Read 1 Corinthians 12:1–11 and consider how the use of your own spiritual gifts is a signpost for others of God's presence in the world.

> *You who turned the water into wine, reveal yourself to me in ways that confirm your abiding presence. Amen.*

Engage the Word

- How would signs of Jesus' glory have helped John's community?

John addressed a community that had to face people who denied that Jesus was the Messiah. To meet this situation, John gave a clear statement of purpose: "Now Jesus did many other signs in the presence of his disciples, which are not written in this book. But these are written so that you may come to believe that Jesus is the Messiah, the Human One, and that through believing you may have life in his name" (John 20:30–31).

What Jesus did at the wedding at Cana was one of those "signs" that led Jesus' disciples to believe in him (note the climax of the story in v. 11). Some sixty years later, John wanted to support and encourage his readers in their belief in Jesus too. Accounts of weddings and wine such as this one were intended to be "epiphany" stories—stories that show forth and reveal God's presence at work.

They celebrate God's power to transform the old into the new and to bring new life to people.

The wedding at Cana proclaimed God's glory, God's presence, at work in Jesus "on the third day" (v. 1). Such a phrase has clear overtones that ring with the proclamation of Jesus' resurrection. John wanted people to read the stories and signs of Jesus' life and ministry through the lens of Jesus' death and resurrection.

The story also brings a disturbing interchange between Jesus and his mother: "Woman, what concern is that to you and to me?" (v. 4). It sounds disrespectful. But what is at stake is the issue of who determines Jesus' work. His mother? No, God. Jesus is clear throughout John that his work is determined by God alone (John 5:17).

The water jars for the rites of purification are another important element in this wedding account. The jars filled with water contrast with the jars filled with wine. The old rites of purification, those represented by the water jars, were no longer in effect. Now Jesus was the purifier, "the Lamb of God who takes away the sin of the world" (John 1:29). The good wine was an epiphany that pointed to Jesus and the revealing of God's glory and presence in him. He came to cleanse and bring new life to all who would believe in him as the one in whom God showed self-giving love.

The wine also suggests the Holy Communion, though there are no words of institution in this Gospel. To drink the wine is to drink that good gift of God's self-giving love in Jesus. To believe in Jesus is not simply to make an intellectual statement about him. It is to enter into and participate in him, to eat and drink, to "taste and see that God is good" (Psalm 34:8), and to celebrate that God has given us the good wine in Jesus.

Respond to the Word

- What can you do, either alone or with companions, to help others identify signposts of God's abiding presence and glory?
- Read "Could I?" and decide what Jesus needs to transform in your life right now. How will you open yourself to let that transformation happen?

Go with the Word

Could I?

> *If Jesus could transform*
> *common water*
>   *into wedding wine*
> *spit and dirt*
>   *into new sight*
> *troubled sea*
>   *into a pathway*
> *well water*
>   *into living water*
> *Could Christ transform*
>   *the waters of my life*
>   *shallow*
>   *murky*
>   *polluted*
>   *stagnant*
>   *sour*
>   *into a shower*
>   *of blessing?*

Tom Lane, "Could I?" in *alive now!* 12, no. 3 (May/June 1982), 51.
Used by permission of the author.

Fulfilled in Your Hearing

Jesus stood up to read, "The Spirit of God is upon me, because God has anointed me to bring good news to the poor, and God has sent me to proclaim release to the captives and recovery of sight to the blind, to let the oppressed go free, to proclaim the year of God's favor." And Jesus rolled up the scroll, gave it back to the attendant, and sat down. The eyes of all in the synagogue were fixed on Jesus, who began to say to them, "Today this scripture has been fulfilled in your hearing."

Luke 4:16c, 18–21

Bible Reading:	Luke 4:14–21
Additional Bible Readings:	Nehemiah 8:1–3, 5–6, 8–10
	Psalm 19
	1 Corinthians 12:12–31a

Enter the Word

- What is your reaction when a long-standing promise is fulfilled?
- In what ways does Jesus fulfill biblical promises?

Visualize yourself seated in the synagogue. Jesus, whom you

remember as a boy, has returned to the synagogue. On this particular Sabbath, he fervently reads familiar passages from Isaiah 61:1–2
and 58:6. Read Luke 4:14–19. Think about how you might respond
now to Jesus, whose parents were your friends.

Read Luke 4:20–21. This "boy" you remember is now seated,
just as a religious teacher would be. Think about how you would
respond to the revealing statement that he made. Imagine what you
would say to other worshipers after the service, as well as what you
would say to Jesus himself.

Write a paraphrase of Luke 4:18–19 to express what Jesus might
say if he were to proclaim this news in your community today.

Find one passage that you would present to your hometown
congregation that describes your call to a ministry of love and justice. Ponder why that scripture is so meaningful to you.

Read Nehemiah 8:1–3, 5–6, and 8–10 and imagine how the
exiles who had returned felt on hearing these words from the law.
As you study Psalm 19, note the references in verses 7–10 to the
life-giving nature of God's law. First Corinthians 12:12–31a speaks
of using one's spiritual gifts to build up the body of Christ.

> *Let me this day fulfill the mission that you have for me,*
> *O God, just as Jesus fulfilled his. Amen.*

Engage the Word

- Why might Luke, who wrote for a Gentile audience, have
  shown Jesus within the context of his own Jewish heritage?

As Luke wrote about Jesus for his community toward the end of
the first century, an important emphasis was Jesus' link to his
Hebrew heritage and Scriptures. Jesus was Jewish, and for early
Christians his ministry fulfilled passages from the Hebrew Scriptures.

The gospel writer expressed this in Luke 4:14–21 by pointing to
Jesus' own quotation from Hebrew Scriptures at the very beginning
of his ministry and by commenting on the risen Jesus' interpretation of Scripture in reference to himself.

Today's reading follows Luke's story of Jesus' baptism (see Luke
3:15–17, 21–22 for Epiphany 1) and temptation. God's Holy Spirit
empowered Jesus for his ministry at his baptism. Filled with the
Holy Spirit, he triumphed over the tempting power of evil that

tried to get him to doubt his identity as God's Child and detour him from his mission.

As Luke continued the story, it is when Jesus was "filled with the power of the Spirit" that he began his ministry of teaching in synagogues in Galilee with a very positive response (vv. 14–15). The Spirit's empowerment of Jesus at his baptism as the agent of God's goodwill for all people began to work.

Luke presented Jesus, as well as his parents, as those who fully observed Jewish customs (Luke 2:21–24, 39, 41). To read from the Isaiah scroll in his hometown synagogue (vv. 16–17) fit into Jesus' life as an observant Jew. The synagogue was a place for prayer and the reading and interpretation of the Hebrew Scriptures (note also today's reading from Nehemiah). Christian worship has followed a pattern similar to that of the synagogue.

For Luke, Jesus' reading from Isaiah became a scriptural base for understanding his mission. Jesus' ministry would fulfill God's mission in ways that the Isaiah text had pointed to some five hundred years earlier. Now the Spirit anointed and empowered him "to bring good news to the poor . . . release to the captives . . . sight to the blind . . . to let the oppressed go free, to proclaim the year of God's favor" (vv. 18–19).

The "year of God's favor" may point to the Year of Jubilee (see Leviticus 25:8–12). It was a year to "proclaim liberty throughout the land to all its inhabitants" (v. 10). Jesus' ministry was to be a liberating ministry to free people from the personal and social bondage that holds them captive.

These texts from Isaiah 58:6 and 61:1–2 originally addressed Israel after the Exile in Babylon. It meant good news to poor and captive, sightless and oppressed people. The same God who was at work in Isaiah's world would now be at work in Jesus' world. Now it was Jesus who was fulfilling God's purpose through the words of Isaiah.

Respond to the Word

- How might you, along with others, work to bring about justice for those who are poor, oppressed, or captive?
- As a follower of Jesus, what will you do today to reflect God's love and justice?

Go with the Word

I Thank You for Those Things That Are Yet Possible

. . .

Thank you
for work
   which engages me in an internal debate
      between right and reward
   and stretches me toward responsibility
      to those who pay for my work,
         and those who cannot pay
            because they have no work;
for justice
   which repairs the devastations of poverty;
for liberty
   which extends to the captives of violence;
for healing
   which binds up the broken bodied
   and the broken hearted;
for bread broken
   for all the hungry earth;
for good news
   of which love is stronger than death;
and for peace
   for all to sit under fig trees
      and not be afraid;
for my calling . . . my life.

. . .

Ted Loder, in *Guerrillas of Grace: Prayers for the Battle* (San Diego: Lura Media, 1984), 43. Copyright © 1984 by Innisfree Press, Inc. Used by permission.

Accept or Reject?

And Jesus said, "Truly I tell you, no prophet is accepted in the prophet's hometown." When they heard this, all in the synagogue were filled with rage. They got up, drove Jesus out of the town, and led him to the brow of the hill on which their town was built, so that they might hurl him off the cliff. But passing through the midst of them, Jesus went away.

Luke 4:24, 28–30

Bible Reading: Luke 4:21–30

Additional Bible Readings: Jeremiah 1:4–10
                                  Psalm 71:1–6
                                  1 Corinthians 13:1–13

Enter the Word

- How does it feel to be accepted? to be rejected?
- How does the content of Jesus' message affect your willingness to accept him?

Begin your study by reading Luke 4:14–30, a passage that includes last week's verses. Make a list across the top of a sheet of paper: Jesus, the congregation, the rabbi, and the few in the congregation who later may have become followers. Under each name write a thought or emotion that may have been experienced during each of the following occurrences:

While Jesus was reading the scripture.
After he said, "This scripture has been fulfilled."
When he said, "No prophet is accepted in the prophet's hometown."
When he spoke about Elijah and Elisha helping Gentiles.
When they forced Jesus to the cliff.
When he walked through their midst.

After completing the list, meditate first on the teachings of Jesus that draw you to him. Then think about the teachings that you would prefer to ignore or reject. Possibly you will recognize within yourself the same ambivalence about accepting Jesus that the people in his hometown felt.

Read the call of Jeremiah (1:4–10), the prayer for deliverance from enemies in Psalm 71:1–6, and Paul's teaching on love in 1 Corinthians 13:1–13. Draw connections among all the passages.

Open my ears, my eyes, my heart, and my mind that I may accept you, O God, and the Anointed One you sent. Amen.

Engage the Word

- How does Luke's portrait of Jesus' early ministry prepare the readers for his death and resurrection?

The first verse of today's reading overlaps the final verse of last week's, showing that the two are linked and that Luke 4:14–30 really is one text. Everything in Luke 4:14–21 is positive, but with the addition of verses 22–30 the whole tone of the text makes a radical shift. People responded to Jesus' ministry not only with joyous acceptance but also with violent rejection.

The response of Jesus' hometown congregation to his reading and interpretation of Isaiah was at first very positive: "All spoke well of him and were amazed at the gracious words that came from his mouth" (v. 22). This son of Joseph, one of their own, was reading and interpreting the Scripture in their synagogue. And how gracious were his words about good news and liberty!

Yet, as Luke tells the story, Jesus knew that the response of some townspeople demonstrated a limited and exclusive understanding of the words of both Isaiah and Jesus. To them the words meant good news and liberty for their own people—not for others.

Their understanding was like that of Jonah, who did not want good things to happen to the people of hated Nineveh.

Jesus knew that when some grasped his expansive and inclusive understanding of Isaiah, they would throw his words back in his face: "Doctor, cure yourself" (v. 23). They apparently resented the good that Jesus had done in another town, Capernaum—a town with many Gentiles, those outside the Jewish faith. Many in his hometown synagogue wanted him to focus on his own people. "No prophet is accepted in the prophet's hometown" (v. 24) was a proverb that applied to Jesus as well as to the prophet Jeremiah (see the reading from Jeremiah for today). One who prophesies ("speaks for" God) and points to God's inclusiveness often knows rejection even by one's own people (note John 1:11).

Jesus spoke as a prophet. He pointed to how God did not always focus on the people of Israel. In the Hebrew Scriptures, God used Elijah to meet the needs of the Sidonese widow at Zarephath (1 Kings 17:1–18:1) and Elisha to help heal the Syrian warrior Naaman (2 Kings 5:1–14), though Sidon and Syria traditionally were Israel's enemies. Isaiah's words about good news and release and liberty were not only for Jesus' own people. They were for all people, including the enemies of Israel (see Luke 6:27). To be true to their own Scriptures, Jesus' hometown congregation needed to understand that.

For Jesus to point to God at work for good among enemies evoked rage from some of the people. They drove him out of town and wanted to hurl him off a cliff. Jesus' ministry met with both acceptance and rejection. Excluded outcasts received him warmly. His words of challenge to those who excluded them, however, met with violent rejection.

His hometown congregation wanted to destroy him, but he passed through the midst of them (v. 30). This incident at the beginning of his ministry foreshadows the end of his ministry with his death and resurrection.

Respond to the Word

- How do groups that you are associated with respond to Jesus?
- How will you demonstrate your acceptance of Jesus and Jesus' teachings in the coming week?

Go with the Word

Rejection

Luke's report brings the starry-eyed Christian
   down to earth with a thud.
It previews something
that will take place often in Jesus' lifetime:
his words will fall on deaf ears.
Nor is rejection of Jesus' message
a phenomenon peculiar to his day alone.
Many centuries later, Thomas Carlyle wrote:
If Jesus were to come today,
people would not crucify him.
They would ask him to dinner,
hear what he had to say,
and make fun of him.
Why haven't 2,000 years changed things?
A high-school boy volunteered his answer:
Why don't I take Jesus' words more seriously?
I guess because if I did,
most of my friends would reject me,
just as many of Jesus' friends rejected him.
And I guess I couldn't take that just now.
Jesus left Nazareth with a deeper awareness of
not only what lay ahead of him,   .
but also what it meant to be a prophet.
To be a prophet meant to expose himself to rejection—
even death.

Mark Link, in *The Seventh Trumpet: The Good News Proclaimed* (Niles, Ill.: Argus Communications, 1978), 70–71. © 1978 Tabor Publishing, a division of RCL Enterprises, Inc. Used by permission.

Do Not Be Afraid

But when Simon Peter saw the boats filled with fish, he fell down at Jesus' knees, saying, "Go away from me, Lord, for I am a sinful person!" Then Jesus said to Simon, "Do not be afraid; from now on you will be catching people." When they had brought their boats to shore, they left everything and followed Jesus.

Luke 5:8, 10b–11

Bible Reading:	Luke 5:1–11
Additional Bible Readings:	Isaiah 6:1–8 (9–13) Psalm 138 1 Corinthians 15:1–11

Enter the Word

- What are some reasons that people feel afraid?
- How are you comforted when you feel afraid?

Today's reading is one long paragraph packed with action, dialogue, and thoughts—both within and between the lines. Imagine that you are in the boat. Try to picture what is happening in each episode as you read Luke 5:1–11.

Now view this whole story through the eyes of Simon Peter. Jot down on a piece of paper where he is and what he is doing, as well as what you imagine he might be thinking as the story progresses.

Next, view the whole story through the eyes of Jesus. Write

why you believe Jesus chose to be there, why he said and did certain things, and what he may have been thinking about Simon, James, John, and the crowd on the shore.

Finally, look at this reading in terms of your personal spiritual journey. Identify your own response to the presence and call of Jesus. Compare your response to that of Simon Peter.

Read Isaiah 6:1–8 (9–13) and 1 Corinthians 15:1–11 to see how God works through people like us to proclaim good news. Psalm 138 reminds us that God is present in fearful situations.

> *Give me courage, O God, in the face of fear, for you*
> *have called and equipped me for the work I am to do.*
> *Amen.*

Engage the Word

- How would the story of Jesus' response to Peter's feelings of inadequacy have helped Luke's first readers?

Luke had a burning passion for the spread of the "good news of great joy for all the people" (Luke 2:10). It was a task that called for many to help. Luke not only told of Jesus' call of the Twelve (Luke 6:12–16) but also gave special attention to many women followers of Jesus. Unlike the other gospel writers, Luke told of Jesus' appointment of seventy more people (Luke 10:1–2). Acts, the second half of his two-part work, is the story of the growing spread of the good news across the Roman Empire.

As Luke wrote of Jesus' call of Simon Peter to catch people, he wanted his community to see something of themselves in the figure of Simon some sixty years after Jesus' ministry. Now they were the ones Jesus was calling. Now they were the ones who were not to be afraid to continue his mission.

As Luke told of Simon's call, he did so in the context of already having shown aspects of Jesus' ministry (chapter 4). Jesus had begun to model his ministry in the healing of Simon's mother-in-law (Luke 4:38–39).

In today's reading, Jesus also modeled a way of calling followers. He did not call Simon to the synagogue. He went to where Simon was in the midst of his daily work of fishing. He gave Simon the dignity of being needed by using Simon's boat to speak to the people.

Simon was having no success in fishing. And he did not think there was any reason to obey Jesus' words to try again. Yet he obeyed. That is Luke's point. No matter what the prior experience in fishing (mission or discipleship) has been, obey Jesus!

Obedience led to such success that "they signaled their partners in the other boat to come and help them" (v. 7). With a boat as an early Christian symbol for the church, one might see here a beginning ecumenical movement of churches sharing in an overwhelming missionary task.

Why after such success did Simon Peter respond as he did: "Go away from me, Lord, for I am a sinful man" (v. 8)? What was Simon's sin? There is no clear answer in the text. Was it the sin of not trusting Jesus' word that there would be a catch? Or was it the sin of trying to escape Jesus' call because Simon felt inadequate? (Also note Isaiah's response to his call in today's reading, Isaiah 6:5, as well as Paul's, 1 Corinthians 15:9.) But Jesus did not go away from Simon. Jesus called Simon regardless of his sin.

Jesus stayed and called Simon to the task of fishing for people; and he told him to "not be afraid" (v. 10). Why not be afraid? Because Simon Peter and others would follow Jesus, be with him, and obey him. Why not be afraid? Because (to use words from the psalm reading for today) God's steadfast love and faithfulness will endure, preserve one in the midst of trouble, and fulfill God's purpose in the ones called (Psalm 138:2, 7, 8). Paul wrote, "By the grace of God I am what I am, and God's grace toward me has not been in vain" (1 Corinthians 15:10).

Jesus does not call people who say, "Look, Jesus, I'm just the right person for the task. I've got what it takes." No, he calls those who are willing to trust in God with their gifts, despite their inadequacies.

Respond to the Word

- How can a group that you belong to bolster those who feel inadequate to face life challenges?
- How will you open yourself to hear God's call this week?

Go with the Word

God's Call: A Responsive Reading

One: A child once dreamed that God called him by name—
"Samuel." Fisher folk from the Galilean Sea once met a young man
who told them to lay aside their nets and follow. A woman, drawing water from a well, once spoke with a prophet whose words sent
her back to town in a rush.

All: I heard the voice of God saying, "Whom shall I send? Who
will go for us?" Then I said, *"Here am I! Send me."*

One: Moses stood before a burning bush, protesting God's call
upon him: "Who am I to go to pharaoh to free the children of
Israel? . . . What will I say when they ask who sent me? . . . O God,
I beg of you, send someone else!"

All: I heard the voice of God saying, "Whom shall I send? Who
will go for us?" Then I said, *"Here am I! Send me."*

One: Mary stood before God's messenger, amazed at the news
she was hearing, "But how is it possible for this to take place? . . .
Yet, I am God's servant. So, let it be done as you have said."

All: I heard the voice of God saying, "Whom shall I send? Who
will go for us?" Then I said, *"Here am I! Send me."*

One: Jeremiah stood in despair before God who had appointed
him a prophet while he was still within his mother's womb:
"Sovereign God! I do not know how to speak to the nations; I am
too young!"

All: I heard the voice of God saying, "Whom shall I send? Who
will go for us?" Then I said, *"Here am I! Send me."*

One: Mary Magdalene stood in joyous tears before the risen
Christ, framing the message she would bring to her grieving companions: "I have seen the [Savior]!"

All: I heard the voice of God saying, "Whom shall I send? Who
will go for us?" Then I said, *"Here am I! Send me."*

Caren L. Caldwell, in *Touch Holiness: Resources for Worship*, ed. Ruth
C. Duck and Maren C. Tirabassi (New York: The Pilgrim Press, 1990),
54. Used by permission.

Blessed Are You

Jesus came down with them and stood on a level place, with a great crowd of the disciples and a great multitude of people from all Judea, Jerusalem, and the coast of Tyre and Sidon. Jesus looked up at the disciples and said: "Blessed are you who are poor, for yours is the dominion of God. Blessed are you who are hungry now, for you will be filled. Blessed are you who weep now, for you will laugh."

Luke 6:17, 20–21

Bible Reading: Luke 6:17–26

Additional Bible Readings: Jeremiah 17:5–10
                                        Psalm 1
                                        1 Corinthians 15:12–20

Enter the Word

- If five people you know were to list their blessings, what might those lists include?
- How do you personally feel blessed?

Think about your community's perceptions about what it means to be blessed or happy. Recall times when you considered these perceptions. Think about ways your perceptions of happiness

104

have changed and the effect that change has had on your life.

Read Luke 6:17–26. Imagine standing before Jesus and hearing these words. Even as you read them now, they might remind you of perceptions that are uncomfortable for you. Recognize how Jesus' teachings turn traditional perceptions upside down. Reexamine your perceptions in light of Jesus' words.

You may also want to compare Luke 6:20–26 with the Beatitudes as found in Matthew 5:1–11. Note that Matthew does not state curses ("woes") as Luke does. Instead, he points out the benefits that come to those who are blessed.

Read Jeremiah 17:5–10 and Psalm 1 to see ways in which God blesses and curses (or brings woe upon) people according to their behavior. First Corinthians 15:12–20 reminds us of the centrality of Christ's resurrection to our faith. Through it, we are blessed.

> *I sometimes get my priorities mixed up, God, and feel blessed by things that do not satisfy. Help me to experience the true blessings of your realm. Amen.*

Engage the Word

- How does the message in Luke 6:17–26 turn upside down the usual perceptions and expectations of Luke's readers?

In his time, Luke challenged the prevailing view that the rich and powerful alone were blessed. He understood Jesus and his message of God's reign as reversing such values of the world. Mary's words in the infancy stories already expressed this idea: "God has brought down the powerful from their thrones, and lifted up the lowly . . . filled the hungry with good things, and sent the rich away empty" (Luke 1:52–53).

Luke did not want his community toward the end of the first century simply to fit into societal and religious structures that often excluded the powerless and exalted the powerful. He wanted them to see that Jesus called them to a revolutionary faith that reached out to lift up those whom others put down. In his ministry Jesus often included in God's reign those whom others, even religious leaders, rejected.

Today's reading from Luke follows Jesus' choosing of the twelve disciples (Luke 6:12–16). With Luke's emphasis on the importance of prayer, he told of Jesus spending the night in prayer on the mountain, a traditional place of God's revelation. In Luke Jesus often opened himself to God in prayer at crucial points in his ministry.

Jesus then came down from the mountain with his disciples to join a multitude of people from a wide geographic area (v. 17). Here Luke emphasized Jesus' universal outreach to all people.

Before Jesus spoke his Sermon on the Plain (in Matthew 5–7 it is the Sermon on the Mount), his God-given power enabled him to heal people of both physical and mental illness (vv. 18–19). Thus Jesus joined together his healing and teaching ministry. His action became the context for his teaching.

Luke then presented Jesus' teaching in terms of four blessings (beatitudes) (vv. 20–23) contrasted with four woes (vv. 24–26). This blessing-and-woe contrast is a pattern present in today's readings from Psalm 1 and Jeremiah 17:5–10 as well as in Deuteronomy 11:26–28. Jesus' teaching turned the world's views upside down.

Usually people see the blessed as persons who are rich and fed, laughing and acclaimed. But Jesus proclaimed the blessed as persons who are poor and hungry, weeping and persecuted. "Blessed are you who are poor, for yours is the realm of God" (v. 20). In contrast he said, "Woe to you who are rich, for you have received your consolation" (v. 24).

The rich already have their hands so full of themselves and their wealth that they have no room for God's reign. The fed and laughing and acclaimed are so caught up in the present in their own good fortune that they are not open to God's gifts of food and laughter and joyous reward for being faithful to the mission of Jesus (v. 22).

Luke wanted people to understand that Jesus pronounced woe on those who make self-gratification the goal of life. He pronounced blessing on those who trust in God's reign now and forever.

Respond to the Word

- How might the world be different if people in your own community lived according to the principles Jesus taught?
- How does Jesus' teaching prompt you to reevaluate and change your own lifestyle and attitudes?

Go with the Word

Blessed

In those moments of self-giving, inmost desire and outward deed overflow together. Our divided selves are made whole, and we experience God's blessing.

It is when we are pushed to the edge of human possibility by our poverty or our grief, by our thirst for righteousness or our search for peace, by our suffering or our love that God meets us. In these moments, which are our perfection and our peace, God comes to us as sure as the taste of salt on our tongues.

Barbara A. Gerlach, *The Things That Make for Peace* (New York: The Pilgrim Press, 1981), 37.

No Strings Attached

Then Joseph said to his brothers, "Come closer to me."

And they came closer. He said, "I am your brother,

Joseph, whom you sold into Egypt. And now do not be

distressed, or angry with yourselves, because you sold

me here; for God sent me before you to preserve life."

Genesis 45:4–5

Bible Reading: Genesis 45:3–11, 15

Additional Bible Readings: Psalm 37:1–11, 39–40
                               1 Corinthians 15:35–38, 42–50
                               Luke 6:27–38

Enter the Word

- When you think of the phrase "strings attached," what images or personal stories come to mind?
- When friends or family have disappointed you, how have you been able to forgive them and move on?

Today's reading from Genesis records Joseph's reconciliation with his brothers. Brainstorm every word, phrase, or idea that comes to mind when you think about the meaning of reconciliation.

Picture any family, relatives, or friends with whom you currently have a relationship of conflict or estrangement. Also picture any group, race, or nation of people with whom your own group, race, or nation currently has a relationship of conflict or estrangement.

With these personal and social relationships in mind, read Genesis 45:3–11, 15.

Imagine all the possible reactions—negative and positive—that Joseph could have had to his brothers. Now reflect on how the story did, in fact, end. Ponder how this story informs your understanding of the meaning and power of reconciliation. Consider how God is working to break down walls between us and others—whether or not we cooperate with God.

Read the other scriptures—Psalm 37:1–11, 39–40; 1 Corinthians 15:35–38, 42–50; and Luke 6:27–38—and try to make connections with Joseph's story. The "Engage the Word" portion will help you create some links.

> *Let me reach out in your gracious love, O God, to be reconciled with others. Amen.*

Engage the Word

- How does the story of Joseph demonstrate God's will for goodness and reconciliation even in the midst of evil?

The story of Joseph (Genesis 37, 39–50) is one of the great stories in the Bible. It involves family and favorites, father and brothers, dreams and jealousy, plotting and revenge, deceit and mourning. It involves economics and politics, lust and lies, unjust imprisonment and interpretation of dreams, plenty and famine, kin and caring. It involves self-revelation and tears, generosity and resettlement, destitution and slavery, blessing and death, fear and forgiveness.

Yet beneath all this is the underlying theme of God at work for good in the midst of all that happens. Joseph's words in today's reading express that theme: "I am your brother . . . whom you sold into Egypt. And now do not be distressed, or angry with yourselves, because you sold me here; for God sent me before you to preserve life" (vv. 4–5; note also v. 7).

Words near the end of the story again powerfully present that theme. Facing fearful brothers, Joseph says, "Do not be afraid! Am I in the place of God? Even though you intended to do harm to me, God intended it for good, in order to preserve a numerous people" (Genesis 50:19–20). Human evil is not the last word. God's work for good is. Death is not the last word. God's power to give new life is (see 1 Corinthians 15:42–43).

What Joseph's brothers began finally ended with Joseph becoming the Pharaoh's prime minister to oversee economic issues in a time of plenty and then in a time of famine. The famine also affected Joseph's father and brothers. It caused them first to seek food in Egypt and finally to become residents there with Joseph's promise to care for them (see vv. 9–11).

In response to his brothers, Joseph did what Jesus called for in Luke: "Love your enemies, do good to those who hate you. . . . Do to others as you would have them do to you. . . . love your enemies, do good . . . and you will be children of the Most High; for God is kind to the ungrateful and the wicked. Be merciful, just as your God is merciful" (Luke 6:27, 31, 35–36). Rather than acting with vengeance against his brothers, Joseph acted with reconciling love.

Psalm 37:3, 5–6, 8 also reflects the theme of working for good. Here, we are called to do good, to commit ourselves to God, to trust in God, and steer clear of anger and worry.

The Joseph story ends with Jacob's whole family safe in Egypt. But their presence there led to their slavery (see Exodus 1:1–11), which later led to God's mighty deed of deliverance from Egyptian bondage in the Exodus, the most important event in Israel's history. But for the Hebrew writers, the God at work in the Exodus was also the God at work for good in what preceded it in the stories of Abraham and Sarah, Isaac and Rebekah, Jacob and Rachel, Joseph and his brothers. Human evil cannot ultimately thwart God's working for human good. God seeks to reconcile broken relationships with healing love.

Respond to the Word

- How can you help groups in conflict to resolve their differences and put past hurts or injustices behind them?
- Whom do you need to forgive with no strings attached? How will you plan to do that in the near future?

Go with the Word

Love Is . . .

Love, like truth and beauty, is concrete. Love is not fundamentally a sweet feeling; not, at heart, a matter of sentiment, attachment, or being "drawn toward." Love is active, effective, a matter of making reciprocal and mutually beneficial relation with one's friends and enemies. Love creates righteousness, or justice, here on earth. To make love is to make justice.

We are not automatic lovers of self, others, world, or God. Love does not just happen. . . . Love is . . . a willingness to be present to others without pretense or guile. Love is a conversion to humanity—a willingness to participate with others in the healing of a broken world and broken lives.

Carter Heyward, *Our Passion for Justice: Images of Power, Sexuality, and Liberation* (New York: The Pilgrim Press, 1984), 88, 186.

Hear and Act

The good person out of the good treasure of the heart produces good, and the evil person out of evil treasure produces evil; for it is out of the abundance of the heart that the mouth speaks.

Luke 6:45

Bible Reading: Luke 6:39–49

Additional Bible Readings: Sirach 27:4–7
     or Isaiah 55:10–13
     Psalm 92:1–4, 12–15
     1 Corinthians 15:51–58

Enter the Word

- What does it mean to "hear and act" as followers of Jesus?
- How does your hearing of God's word call you to act?

If possible, look at your calendar or spiritual journal. Try to identify recent actions that reflect the example you have seen in Jesus or learned about through his teaching. For example, the parable of the good Samaritan may have prompted you to help a stranded motorist. On a sheet of paper, make a list of your actions in one column and a list of related teachings or actions of Jesus in another column. Read Luke 6:39–49. Then prayerfully consider how your actions can better reflect the gospel you have heard.

Also study the additional readings. Sirach 27:4–7 reveals how actions are the test of a person's character and shortcomings. Isaiah 55:10–13 looks at how God's Word acts to accomplish God's purpose. Psalm 92:1–4, 12–15 gives thanks to God and points out how righteous persons—those who act according to God's will—flourish and produce fruit. First Corinthians 15:51–58 describes God's resurrecting action that enables us to overcome death.

I have heard your words, O God. Now empower me to
act on them according to your will. Amen.

Engage the Word

- What does Luke want his readers to learn from Jesus' example as a teacher?

Today's reading from Luke 6:39–49 is part of Luke's presentation of the Sermon on the Plain (part of which is similar to the Sermon on the Mount in Matthew 5–7). It emphasizes Jesus' role as teacher and calls Jesus' disciples to be like their teacher (v. 40).

Jesus often used familiar images to make his point. In today's passage he speaks of a person who was blind, a speck and a log, good and bad trees and their fruits, houses built on solid rock and soft ground. Jesus apparently knew that many people are visual learners and images helped them not only to hear but to see what he wanted to teach them.

Can a person without sight guide another person without sight (v. 39)? Can someone who does not know God's loving purpose guide others who do not know it? For Luke, Jesus is the teacher who sees and knows God's loving will. Luke calls his hearers late in the first century to learn from Jesus and become "fully qualified" to act on his example (v. 40).

Part of that hearing involves *self*-criticism, before any attempt to criticize others: to see the log in one's own eye before one tries to remove the speck in a neighbor's eye. To do otherwise is to be a hypocrite (vv. 41–42). In Luke's Gospel, Jesus chastises religious leaders for their hypocrisy (12:1).

Jesus teaches that what a person *does* stems from what that person *is*. Bad trees bear bad fruit and good trees bear good fruit (vv. 43–44). Today's reading from Psalm 92 also speaks of righteous people as trees that produce good fruit (vv. 12–15).

It is not a matter simply of what the mouth speaks, but of the good that is treasured in the heart (v. 45). The inner motivation for how we speak and act is crucial. Paul writes to the Corinthians, "If I speak in the tongues of mortals and of angels, but do not have love, I am a noisy gong or a clanging cymbal" (1 Corinthians 13:1).

Simply to *mouth* a confession of Jesus as Sovereign without *doing* what he teaches is meaningless. Someone who comes to Jesus, hears his words, and acts on them is like one who builds a house on a rock that can withstand the floods of life. But one who hears and does not act builds a house on soft ground that ends in ruin (vv. 46–49).

Jesus' words and teaching intend to be like God's word in today's reading from Isaiah 55: "So shall my word be that goes out from my mouth; it shall not return to me empty, but it shall accomplish that which I purpose, and succeed in the thing for which I sent it" (v. 11).

For Luke, that word of God is at work in the words and teaching of Jesus, to be heard and acted upon in the context of the Roman Empire in the late first century. Luke wants his community to give a good account of their faith in Jesus as Sovereign in how they act. He wants for people throughout the Empire to know that Jesus is indeed "good news of great joy for all the people" (Luke 2:10; see also Isaiah 55:12).

In our world today that knows much phony religion, Luke invites us to live out our Christian faith in ways that are convincing. He calls us to hear and act on such words of Jesus as, "Love your enemies, do good to those who hate you, bless those who curse you, pray for those who abuse you. . . . Do to others as you would have them do to you" (Luke 6:27–28, 31).

Respond to the Word

- How can you and your community act as role models and teachers for others?
- What changes do you need to make in order to create a firmer spiritual foundation that will withstand the floods of life?

Go with the Word

Confession

You asked for my hands
that you could use them for your purpose.
I gave them for a moment, then withdrew them
for the work was hard.

You asked for my mouth
to speak against injustice.
I gave you a whisper that I might not be accused.

You asked for my eyes
to see the pain of poverty.
I closed them for I did not want to see.

You asked for my life
that you might work through me.
I gave you a small part that I might not get too involved.

Lord, forgive me for my calculated efforts to serve you
only when it is convenient to do so,
only in places where it is safe to do so,
and only with those who make it easy to do so.

Lord, forgive me,
renew me,
send me out
as a usable instrument
that I may take seriously
the meaning of your cross.

Joe Sermane, in *Bread of Tomorrow: Prayers for the Church Year*, ed. Janet Morley
(Maryknoll, N.Y.: Orbis Books, 1992), 76. Copyright © Joe Sermane.

If you do not observe Transfiguration Sunday, use the session for Proper 4
(page 186) next week.

Transfigured

Jesus took with him Peter and John and James, and went up on the mountain to pray. And while Jesus was praying, the appearance of his face changed, and his clothes became dazzling white. Then from the cloud came a voice that said, "This is my Child, my Chosen; to this one you shall listen!" When the voice had spoken, Jesus was found alone. And they kept silent and in those days told no one of the things they had seen.

Luke 9:28b–29, 35–36

Bible Reading:	Luke 9:28–36 (37–43)
Additional Bible Readings:	Exodus 34:29–35
	Psalm 99
	2 Corinthians 3:12–4:2

Enter the Word

- How might new experiences change people's perspectives?
- How have "mountaintop" experiences enriched your life?

Begin your study of Jesus' transfiguration by recalling and reflecting on your own peak experiences, those mountaintop moments when you felt a profound closeness to God, caught a glimpse of your life's mission and meaning, felt affirmed as God's precious creation, felt the truth of your faith and were filled with energy to live it. List these experiences.

Choose three of these experiences that had the greatest impact on you. Write one paragraph about each of the chosen experiences. Discuss how they changed you and connected you to the holy. Recall whatever you saw or heard or felt in those moments that gave you direction or a lesson in ultimate value.

Read Luke 9:28–36 (37–43), the story of Jesus' transfiguration and discover the impact this event had on Jesus' closest followers.

Read another account of transfiguration in Exodus 34:29–35 and compare it to the story in Luke. Look at the transfiguration images in 2 Corinthians 3:12–4:2. Study Psalm 99 and imagine hearing God speak to you in a pillar of cloud.

> *Let me see your radiant face, O God, that I may be energized to serve you as a more faithful disciple. Amen.*

Engage the Word

- What might this passage tell Luke's community about God's relationship to them?

In the Bible, mountains are places of God's revelation. This is true in the Exodus reading for today, where God is revealed to Moses, and in the passage from Luke, where Jesus and the apostles hear the voice of God. The figure of Moses occurs in all the readings for today, each interpreting something of the revelation of God's glory and presence. Luke 9:28–36 (37–43) has deep roots in the Hebrew Scriptures' witness to God's revealing action.

The mountain in Luke is not only something geographical; it is also a literary high point. This high point in Luke looks back on Jesus' prior ministry and looks forward to his journey to Jerusalem and his suffering, death, and resurrection (see v. 31). It follows Jesus' first prediction of his passion and explanation of discipleship (Luke 9:18–27). It proclaims that he who will suffer is the very one in whom God's glory is present.

Just as in Jesus' baptism God declared him to be the Beloved Child (Luke 3:22), so now again on the mountain God declared him to be chosen (Luke 9:35). And just as at Jesus' baptism where Luke depicted Jesus as praying, opening himself to God, here too Luke presents Jesus as praying.

Luke's community could read what follows knowing that God was not absent from Jesus in his suffering but present in the midst of it. This was affirmed by God not only in words but by the presence of Moses and Elijah (v. 30). For Luke, Moses and Elijah were not just key historical persons in Israel's history. Their names also stood for the law and the prophets, the Hebrew Scriptures (see also Luke 24:25–27, 44–46). The Greek word translated as "departure" (Luke 9:31) is *exodus*. It connects Israel's liberation from Egypt to God's liberating deed in Jesus' death and resurrection.

In the story, Jesus had three disciples with him on the mountain (v. 28). They represented not only themselves but also the community of Jesus' followers. They were sleepy, but they stayed awake for this mountaintop experience. What happened was a witness to them and to Luke's readers sixty years later.

Peter wanted to make that mountaintop experience permanent (v. 33). But at that point a cloud overshadowed them and out of that cloud came God's voice: "This is my Child, my Chosen; listen to him!" (v. 35). They then were alone with Jesus. Such an overwhelming experience did not produce more talk, but silence (v. 36). The time would come when they would proclaim, but the first response to this glorified revelation of God in Jesus was silence.

To heed the command to "listen to him" did not mean staying on the mountain. It meant accompanying Jesus down the mountain to meet the cry of the father for his son who had epilepsy (vv. 37–43). The glory of God is not something to be captured and held for one's own enjoyment. In listening to Jesus, it is a glory that has to meet human need, face suffering for God's healing purpose, and finally know God's liberating exodus from death.

Respond to the Word

- What impact would a glimpse of the transfigured Jesus have on your family, co-workers, or community of faith?
- How will you respond to transfiguring moments in your own life this week?

Go with the Word

Living by Vision

Transfiguration is living by vision: standing foursquare in the midst of a broken, tortured, oppressed, starving, dehumanizing reality, yet seeing the invisible, calling to it to come, behaving as if it is on the way, sustained by elements of it that have come already, within and among us. In those moments when people *are* healed, transformed, freed from addictions, obsessions, destructiveness, self worship or when groups or committees or even, rarely, whole nations glimpse the light of the transcendent in their midst, there the New Creation has come upon us. The world for one brief moment is transfigured. The beyond shines in our midst—on the way to the cross.

Walter Wink, "Expository Article on Mark 9:2–8," *Interpretation: A Journal of Bible and Theology* 36 (1982): 63.

Rembrandt Harmensz van Rijn, *Return of the Prodigal Son*, 1668–69, oil on canvas, 262 x 205 cm., The Hermitage Museum, St. Petersburg, Russia (Scala/Art Resource, N.Y.). Used by permission.

Lent

On Ash Wednesday Christians begin the spiritual journey of Lent that extends for forty days through the night before Easter. During this period of self-examination, you are reminded of who you are and whose you are. You confront your own shortcomings and repent of your failure to be what God has created and called you to be. While Lent is a time of intense reflection, both individually and collectively, it is also a time of hope as you explore possibilities for new beginnings.

Rembrandt's painting *Return of the Prodigal Son* captures the transformation that occurs when one returns to God. As you look at this painting, consider your own need to kneel before the compassionate Parent and experience the grace of unconditional love and forgiveness.

Although the main liturgical color for Lent is purple, the season begins with black or gray on Ash Wednesday, colors that signify mortality and mourning. For Palm Sunday, punctuated by joyous shouts of "Hosanna" as Jesus rides into Jerusalem, the color red adorns the church. On Maundy Thursday, the night of the Passover and Jesus' last meal with the disciples, the color is again purple. Just as the season began with black, so it ends on Good Friday as Christians recall the Crucifixion.

Meeting Temptation

Jesus, full of the Holy Spirit, returned from the Jordan and was led by the Spirit in the wilderness, where for forty days he was tempted by the devil.

Luke 4:1–2a

Bible Reading: Luke 4:1–13

Additional Bible Readings: Deuteronomy 26:1–11
Psalm 91:1–2, 9–16
Romans 10:8b–13

Enter the Word

- How do you define "temptation"?
- What temptations have you faced recently?

Read Luke 4:1–13, noting any key words or phrases that seem important to you.

Think about what tempts you, where you meet temptation, and how your faith helps you respond to temptation. Return to the key words and phrases that you noted from the reading. Consider how your experiences of temptation are similar to and different from those of Jesus. Explore connections you have found between your experiences of temptation and Jesus' experience.

Recall words you have said in response to temptations. Notice in Luke 4:4, 8, and 12 that Jesus used words from Deuteronomy to answer the tempter's offerings. Look for ideas in Jesus' words that could help you respond to temptation. Visualize yourself in a tempting situation and play over in your mind how you might respond to it.

Continue your study by reading Deuteronomy 26:1–11, a liturgy for use as first fruits are presented in the central sanctuary, which includes an affirmation of who the people are in relation to God. Romans 10:8b–13 concerns affirmation of the Christian's identity. Read alongside of Luke 4:11, Psalm 91:1–2 and 9–16 reminds us that even the devil can quote scripture.

> *You who have met and conquered temptation, help me to avoid the tempter's snare that I may be true to you. Amen.*

Engage the Word

- As Luke understood it, what was the purpose of Jesus' temptation in the wilderness?

Luke's story of Jesus' temptation, written for Luke's community some fifty or sixty years after Jesus, follows the story of Jesus' baptism as God's Child (Luke 3:21–22) and a genealogy that links him to God's child Adam ("humanity," Luke 3:23–38). God's Holy Spirit empowered Jesus at his baptism for his mission to all of God's sons and daughters.

One might think that being empowered by the Spirit, Jesus could avoid temptation. But it is precisely Jesus, "full of the Holy Spirit," who was led by the Spirit to face temptation (vv. 1–2). To be empowered means to have the ability to confront the evil that tempts, not to avoid it.

For biblical writers like Luke, evil was real. The words "satan" (from the Hebrew) and "devil" (from the Greek) personify that evil and point to how real and personal the evil forces in human experience were for these writers. Jesus, empowered by God's Spirit, did face real opposition.

Luke's setting (Jesus in the wilderness for forty days) has parallels in Moses' forty days without food (Deuteronomy 9:9) and Israel's forty years of trial in the wilderness. (Forty is a sacred biblical number signifying a long period.) In his temptation, Jesus also quotes from Deuteronomy three times to counter the Devil. New Testament writers like Luke often see parallels in Jesus' experience and that of Israel; Israel's Scripture was Jesus' Scripture. Luke wanted his community to see that connection.

What is Jesus' basic temptation? The temptation to doubt who he is lies beneath the three specific temptations: to turn stone to bread (Jesus was hungry); to have glory and authority over the world; and to trust God to save one from foolhardy action.

Twice the Devil says, "If you are the Child of God . . ." (vv. 3, 9). God proclaimed Jesus' identity in his baptism: "You are my Child" (Luke 3:22). To doubt that identity and succumb to the Devil's temptation would lead to identifying himself in terms of material possessions, worldly power and glory, and foolish religion. In turn, he would lose his identity as God's Child and shift his loyalty from God to the Devil.

Jesus affirms his identity and his loyalty to God with the three quotations from Deuteronomy to meet each temptation (Deuteronomy 8:3, 6:13, 6:16; note also that the Devil can misuse scripture). To know one's identity as God's child is the way to meet temptation.

In one reading for today, Israel told its history in order to affirm its identity as God's people (see Deuteronomy 26:5–9). In another, Christians confessed who they are with the words "Jesus is Sovereign" (Romans 10:9–10). These creedal statements are constant reminders to God's people of who they are in the midst of the world's temptation.

In his baptism, Jesus heard, "You are my Child." In baptism, God says to the baptized, "You are my child." That gift of recognition by God, empowered by the Spirit, enables us to confront evil and not succumb to the tempting false identities of material things or power or of being falsely "religious."

Respond to the Word

- How can you and other adults empower younger Christians to be faithful to their identity in the face of temptation?
- When confronted by a tempting situation, what can you do this week to affirm your own identity as God's child?

Go with the Word

Choices

The choice between God and every other god is a real choice. Both make promises, both demand loyalty. It is possible to live by both. If there were no real alternative to God, all [humanity] would choose [God]. Indeed, God is the more difficult choice to justify in terms of provable results.

The chief difficulty is that God demands of us that we live by faith: faith in [God], [God's] sovereignty over the future, [God's] sufficiency for the present; while, on the other hand, the various other gods whom we can serve appeal to us in terms of the things which we can see and the forces which we can calculate. The choice between the life of faith and the life of sight is a choice between a God whom only faith can apprehend and gods whom one has only to see to understand.

D. T. Niles, in *The Bible Through Asian Eyes*, ed. Masao Takenaka and Ron O'Grady (Auckland, New Zealand: Pace Publishing in association with The Asian Christian Art Association, 1991), 90.

Challenged

Jesus said, "Jerusalem, Jerusalem, the city that kills the prophets and stones those who are sent to it! How often have I desired to gather your children together as a hen gathers her brood under her wings, and you were not willing!"

Luke 13:34

Bible Reading: Luke 13:31–35

Additional Bible Readings: Genesis 15:1–12, 17–18
Psalm 27
Philippians 3:17–4:1
Luke 9:28–36

Enter the Word

- How does Jesus challenge people?
- What is challenging you right now?

Read Luke 13:31–35, saying aloud the words that Jesus said (vv. 32b–35). Try two or three readings with different voices, emphases, and volumes. Don't worry about how you think Jesus might have sounded. Simply hear the challenge in Jesus' words.

Focus on verse 34. This powerful image is captured in the art on page 129. As you ponder both Luke's words and Kollwitz's art, think of the ways you identify with this image. Name those whom you have tried to take under your own wing.

Reflect on your emotional response to Luke 13:31–35. Recall

126

feelings you have had, perhaps concerning a loved one, similar to those that Jesus had about Jerusalem. Note that although Jesus' words sound as if he were exasperated, he does not give up on Jerusalem. In fact, he heals a man in the verses after today's reading. Possibly his actions will encourage you as you face a situation where someone refuses your loving concern.

Read Luke 13:31–35 again. This time look for the source of Jesus' strength and enthusiasm in meeting the challenges of a leader. Think about ways in which Jesus' words inform your leadership in whatever arenas you serve.

Read the passage one more time. Substitute the name of your community for "Jerusalem." Think about the challenges that Jesus would issue to you and your neighbors today.

Read Genesis 15:1–12 and 17–18, in which God challenges Abraham and Sarah to a seemingly impossible vision. Philippians 3:17–4:1 records Paul's challenge to live a Christian life, while Psalm 27 recalls the psalmist's challenge from enemies. Luke 9:28–36 records the challenge of changed perspective.

> *Challenge me, O God, to live as a faithful disciple in your realm of love, peace, and justice. Amen.*

Engage the Word

- What impact might Jesus' challenge have had on Luke's community?

What challenged Jesus in his ministry? Luke proclaimed that people's needs challenged Jesus: needs of those sick in body or mind, of the hungry and poor, of the fearful and lost, of those whom others rejected and excluded. He met the challenge to reach out to them with healing and hope as the servant of God's reign of justice and love and peace.

But as he met such challenges, some political and religious leaders challenged and opposed him. His mercy threatened their might. His compassion broke the barriers they wanted to maintain. His truth exposed their hypocrisy. This was not something new. The same kind of thing had happened for centuries.

The reading from Luke 13 tells of opposition to Jesus. It is part of the story of Jesus' journey to Jerusalem (Luke 9:51–19:28): "He set his face to go to Jerusalem" (Luke 9:51). Luke 13:35 points to his entry into Jerusalem (see Luke 19:38). Jerusalem as a political and religious center was central to Luke. In Jerusalem, Jesus' ministry ended (in Luke) and the church's mission began (in Acts).

The reading points first to Herod (Herod Antipas, king under the Romans and son of Herod the Great, king when Jesus was born), who had killed John the Baptist (Luke 9:9). Then he wanted to kill Jesus (later he killed Jesus' disciple James, Acts 12:2). But some members of the devout Pharisees warned Jesus. Jesus responded, "Go and tell that fox for me, 'Listen, I am casting out demons and performing cures today and tomorrow, and on the third day I finish my work.' " Jesus continued to meet the challenge to heal, and the whole story would end "on the third day" (a phrase that points to Jesus' resurrection; see Luke 9:22, 18:33).

But before resurrection, Jesus' death would occur in Jerusalem—a city that had seen the death of prophets before (v. 34). It was a place whose children (people) Jesus wanted to gather "as a hen gathers her brood under her wings"; but they refused. So Jerusalem was left to its own end (v. 35). Jesus finally wept over the city because they did not know "the things that make for peace" (Luke 19:41–44).

For Luke, the very ones who accept the challenge to heal human hurts and promote public peace are challenged and even killed by those who want to maintain their possessions and power and prestige. This challenge happened to the psalmist (Psalm 27:2–3; read the whole psalm). It happened to John the Baptist. It happened to Jesus. It happened to James. It happened to Paul. It still happens to people in many places in today's world.

Yet the words of the psalmist, "God is my light and my salvation; whom shall I fear?" (Psalm 27:1), are a reminder of the hope and abiding faith of those who meet the challenge.

Respond to the Word

- How can you help others meet the challenges of discipleship?
- How might Jesus' words in Luke empower you to face the challenges you need to wrestle with this week?

Go with the Word

How does this image of a woman with her children remind you of Jesus' love for humanity?

Käthe Kollwitz, *Seed Corn Must Not Be Ground,*
© 1997 Artists Rights Society (ARS), New York/VG
Bild-Kunst, Bonn, Germany. Used by permission.

F r e e   t o   R e j o i c e

Now Jesus was teaching in one of the synagogues on the sabbath. And just then there appeared a woman with a spirit that had crippled her for eighteen years. She was bent over and was quite unable to stand up straight. When Jesus saw her, he called her over and said, "Woman, you are set free from your ailment." When he laid his hands on her, immediately she stood up straight and began praising God.

Luke 13:10–13

Bible Reading:	Luke 13:10–17
Additional Bible Readings:	Isaiah 55:1–9
	Psalm 63:1–8
	1 Corinthians 10:1–13
	Luke 13:1–9

Enter the Word

- What are some reasons for rejoicing?
- From what do you need to be freed in your own life?

Sit quietly and begin breathing deeply and slowly. When you have had enough time to calm yourself, think about how you feel right now. Pinpoint the place(s) where your body hurts. Touch them if you can. Also focus on any spiritual pain, such as hurt feelings or broken relationships, you might be experiencing. Pray that God will heal you. Hear Jesus say, "You are set free from your ailment." Praise God in whatever way is appropriate for you.

Now read Luke 13:10–17. Consider ways in which you and the woman are alike. Hear Jesus' words, "Woman, you are set free from your ailment," first from her perspective. Imagine how you would feel and what you would say. Now hear these liberating words from the point of view of the religious leaders who wanted to preserve the sanctity of the Sabbath. Again, imagine what you would say. Finally, hear Jesus' words of release from the vantage point of the other worshipers. Ponder your own response to Jesus, who could heal a long-standing infirmity with a few words.

Read today's additional scriptures. Isaiah 55:1–9 invites you to seek God now, for you will receive mercy and pardon. In Psalm 63:1–8 the psalmist writes about how he has sought God and sung for joy. Paul issues a warning in 1 Corinthians 10:1–13 against overconfidence. Luke 13:1–9 records a call by Jesus for repentance. Draw your own connections between these passages and Luke 13:10–17.

> *Liberating Healer, release me from the ills that bind me so that I might be free to rejoice in praise to you. Amen.*

Engage the Word

- How does Jesus' power to free, to feed, and to heal release people to experience new life?

In the Gospels people often praise and rejoice because of what God has done in Jesus to help, heal, and free them for new life. Luke 13:10–17 tells of one such event. While Jesus was teaching in a synagogue on the Sabbath, a woman appeared who had been crippled, bent over, and unable to stand up straight for eighteen years. Often such people were shunned, even regarded as sinners whose wrongdoing had caused their condition. But Jesus saw the woman, spoke to her, touched her, and freed her to stand straight. Then she began praising God.

Apparently her condition was more than simply physical. The reading speaks about "a spirit that had crippled her" (v. 11) and sees her as one "whom Satan bound" (v. 16). People in both Jesus' time and Luke's time knew that one's inner life can affect one's outer condition and that the impact of evil forces (personified by Satan) can "cripple" people both within and without. Jesus' out-reaching recognition, word, and touch broke the effect of such crip-pling "spirits" and freed people to "stand up straight."

In the reading, it seems that everyone would want to rejoice. But a religious leader objected. According to some religious rules, there was to be no healing on the Sabbath, no "work." Jesus chal-lenged the hypocrisy that allowed work to tend an animal but not work to heal a person (v. 15; Luke 14:1–5), especially since the Sabbath was a day for renewal and healing.

Jesus spoke of the healed woman as "a daughter of Abraham." In that patriarchal culture, emphases fell more on the "sons" of Abraham. Here Jesus included this woman in the promise of bless-ing to Abraham (Genesis 12:3). (Among the Gospels, this story appears only in Luke, which puts great emphasis on women.)

Jesus' response about Sabbath healing shamed his opponents, and the entire crowd rejoiced "at all the wonderful things that he was doing" (v. 17). Earlier in the story, the woman praised God (v. 13). In her rejoicing she could have joined with the psalmist in today's reading: "For you have been my help, and in the shadow of your wings I sing for joy" (Psalm 63:7).

Her individual rejoicing turned into community rejoicing. Praise and rejoicing are never a matter only for the one set free for a new life of "standing straight." Individual and community belong togeth-er. As Paul puts it, "Rejoice with those who rejoice" (Romans 12:15).

Respond to the Word

- How can you work with others to free people from physical, mental, social, economic, or spiritual "ailments" that have bound them?
- From what has God already freed you? Offer praise for that freedom right now.

Go with the Word

O Glad, Exulting, Culminating Song!

A vigor more than earth's is thy notes . . .
A reborn race appears—a perfect world, all joy!
Women and men in wisdom, innocence and health—all joy!
Riotous laughing bacchanals fill'd with joy!

War, sorrow, suffering gone—
*   the rank earth purged—nothing but joy left!*

The ocean fill'd with joy—the atmosphere all joy!

Joy! joy in freedom, worship, love!
*   joy in the ecstasy of life!*

Enough to merely be! enough to breathe!

Joy! joy! all over joy!

Walt Whitman, as quoted in Mark Link, In the Stillness Is the Dancing
(Niles, Ill.: Argus Communications, 1972), 119.

Welcome Home

So the younger son set off and went to his father. But while he was still far off, his father saw him and was filled with compassion; he ran and put his arms around him and kissed him.

Luke 15:20

Bible Reading:	Luke 15:1–3, 11b–32
Additional Bible Readings:	Joshua 5:9–12
	Psalm 32
	2 Corinthians 5:16–21

Enter the Word

- What makes a place home?
- How do you feel about returning to your childhood home, if such a return is possible for you now?

This week's reading is a familiar parable from Luke 15:1–3, 11b–32, often called the parable of the prodigal son or forgiving father. Read this story with "fresh eyes," noticing details or ideas that you have previously overlooked.

Put yourself in the place of each character in the story. Try to understand each character's point of view and feel what each of them feels. If you could be only one of the characters in the story, decide which you would be. Drawing on the connections you make with this story, explore the reasons why you identify with the character you chose.

Now imagine yourself as one of the original hearers of this

story. Think about how your perceptions of your relationship with God would have been turned upside down, whether you were one of the sinners or one of the religious leaders.

Examine your own life. Perhaps there are reasons that you need to "return home," to ask for forgiveness and a second chance. Think of situations that might prompt you to "go back home." Describe what prevents you from going back now.

Possibly the home you want to return to is a church home. Explore reasons why you may have left a particular congregation or feel as if you are on the fringes. Consider steps you can take to return to that community of faith or locate a new one.

Read the additional scriptures for this week. Joshua 5:9–12 records the celebration of the first Passover in the Hebrews' new home, Israel. Psalm 32, which praises God for healing, speaks of God as a "hiding place," a kind of home for the psalmist. 2 Corinthians 5:16–21 refers to those who are in Christ as new creatures, just as the reconciled prodigal was a new creature.

> *Welcoming God, I thank you for flinging wide the doors of your home that I may enter in and experience your forgiving love. Amen.*

Engage the Word

- What reactions might the members of Luke's Gentile community have had to this parable?

As one of several parables found only in Luke, Jesus' parable of the compassionate father emphasizes what Luke wanted for his community. Parables do not so much clarify a point as confront the hearer and invite a change. That is why it is important to note Jesus' audience for the parable, two very separate groups: tax collectors and sinners, Pharisees and scribes—religious outsiders and religious insiders (vv. 1–3). In which character would Luke's community see themselves? In the waiting father? In the "lost" son? In the brother unwilling to celebrate?

The two previous parables (vv. 3–10) portray a "seeking" shepherd and a "seeking" woman. Today's parable portrays a "waiting father." He lets the younger son go (even gives him his inheritance in advance) and does not go after him. He waits until the son "came to himself" (v. 17). The son then wants to go back, confess his sin, and ask to become a hired hand.

The father sees him coming, is "filled with compassion," runs, embraces, and kisses him (v. 20). The son can say only part of what he planned to say (he never gets to the "hired hand" part) before the father calls for a celebration to welcome him home. Did the tax collectors and sinners see themselves in that son?

The father had an elder son to whom the rest of the inheritance belonged ("all that is mine is yours," said the father in verse 31). The elder brother was "angry and refused to go in" (v. 28). He would not even call his brother "brother." He speaks to his father of "this son of yours" (v. 30). For him, the homecoming of such a brother deserved fasting, not feasting; a penalty, not a party; mourning, not merrymaking. Did the religious authorities see themselves in the elder son?

In Luke's time, fifty or sixty years after Jesus told the parable, Luke may have wanted societal outcasts to see themselves as the younger son, now welcomed home by the waiting, compassionate God of Israel. He may have wanted the good, religious folk of his time to come to the party held in honor of the forgiven and those who had been outsiders.

The other readings for this week echo the theme of a forgiving and reconciling God. The psalm declares, "Happy are those whose transgression is forgiven [let go]" (Psalm 32:1). And Paul proclaimed to the Corinthians that "in Christ God was reconciling the world to God's self, not counting their trespasses against them" (2 Corinthians 5:19).

Respond to the Word

- How can you, as a member of a family or church, reach out to and welcome someone who has been estranged and encourage that person to return?
- How has God welcomed you with compassion? How can you, in turn, welcome someone who, like the prodigal, does not "deserve" to be welcomed?

Go with the Word

Leaving Home

More than any other story in the Gospel, the parable of the prodigal son expresses the boundlessness of God's compassionate love. And when I place myself in that story under the light of that divine love, it becomes painfully clear that leaving home is much closer to my spiritual experience than I might have thought. . . .

Leaving home is . . . much more than an historical event bound to time and place. It is a denial of the spiritual reality that I belong to God with every part of my being, that God holds me safe in an eternal embrace, that I am indeed carved in the palms of God's hands and hidden in their shadows. Leaving home means ignoring the truth that God has "fashioned me in secret, moulded me in the depths of the earth and knitted me together in my mother's womb." Leaving home is living as though I do not yet have a home and must look far and wide to find one.

Henri J. M. Nouwen, *The Return of the Prodigal Son: A Meditation of Fathers, Brothers, and Sons* (New York: Doubleday, 1992), 33, 35.

Jesus or the Poor?

Mary took a pound of costly perfume made of pure nard, anointed Jesus' feet, and wiped them with her hair. The house was filled with the fragrance of the perfume. But Judas Iscariot, one of the disciples (the one who was about to betray Jesus), said, "Why was this perfume not sold for thousands of dollars and the money given to the poor?" Jesus said, "Leave her alone. She bought it so that she might keep it for the day of my burial. You always have the poor with you, but you do not always have me."

John 12:3–5, 7–8

Bible Reading:	John 12:1–8
Additional Bible Readings:	Isaiah 43:16–21
	Psalm 126
	Philippians 3:4b–14

Enter the Word

- How do you think God expects the poor to be treated?
- What are you willing to do to show your devotion to Jesus?

Envision yourself at a dinner party or family gathering where Jesus is present. Imagine who else is there; smell and taste the food; listen to the conversation and laughter. Reflect on how your life might be different because you were in the presence of Jesus.

Now read John 12:1–8, which records the events of a dinner given for Jesus at Bethany in the home of Lazarus. As you read, put yourself in the place of each person in the story. Try to understand each one's perspective. Ponder the way in which this encounter transformed the lives of those present.

Explore your own response to the story and to the characters. See yourself as Mary and then as Judas. Consider how Jesus would have responded to you had you been there.

Examine your own devotion to Christ and where this devotion has led you. Consider the ways in which you minister to the needs of others and to your own needs. Think about the kinds of gifts you give to others in Jesus' name.

Continue your study by reading Isaiah 43:16–21, which speaks of God doing a "new thing." Psalm 126 is a prayer asking God to favor the people as in former times. In Philippians 3:4b–14 Paul writes of the supreme value that Jesus has for him. Try to make connections between these readings and John 12.

> Let me be extravagant in my devotion to you, O God, just as Jesus was extravagant in his life-giving service to me. Amen.

Engage the Word

- How might this story have helped John's readers connect loving service to others with their relationship to Jesus?

The John reading occurs in a setting that moves toward Passover and Jesus' death. In John's Gospel, Jesus died as the Lamb of God (John 1:29, 36) on the Day of Preparation as the Passover lambs were slaughtered (John 19:14).

Mary (the sister of Martha and Lazarus, whose raising triggered the final plot against Jesus; see John 11:45–53) performs a beautiful act of anointing Jesus' feet with costly perfume—an anointing that anticipates Jesus' burial (v. 7).

Judas, the disciple of Jesus who betrayed him, objected. He

spoke of selling the perfume and giving the money to the poor, but his true motive was quite different (see v. 6). This suggests that betrayers and thieves are not necessarily outsiders. They can be insiders who have let their greed corrupt them.

Jesus defends Mary's deed and, anticipating his death, Jesus says, "You always have the poor with you, but you do not always have me" (v. 8). By such words Jesus did not intend to set up an either/or situation—either the poor or me. Rather, he described a both/and state—both the poor and me.

In the context of John's Gospel, which proclaims Jesus' death as the deepest expression of God's love for the world (John 3:16), Mary's anointing really points to God's love for all. Her deed does not diminish a concern for the poor. Rather, it heightens it by celebrating God's self-giving love (note John 3:17–18).

What Mary did filled her home with the fragrance of the perfume, but this act pointed beyond to a love in Jesus' death/burial that was to fill the whole world with its saving fragrance. Paul wrote about what God has done in Jesus as "a fragrance from life to life" (2 Corinthians 2:16).

The Isaiah reading points to God's past deed in freeing Israel from Egyptian bondage (Isaiah 43:16–17), as well as to the future deed God is about to do to make a way home from Exile in Babylon. God has performed another "new deed" in Jesus. In the Philippians reading, Paul speaks about "the surpassing value of knowing Christ Jesus my Lord" (Philippians 3:8).

To celebrate God's love in Jesus is precisely to know a love that includes the poor. Jesus said, "I give you a new commandment, that you love one another . . . as I have loved you" (John 13:34).

Respond to the Word

- What steps can you, along with other persons, take to change an unjust system that oppresses the poor?
- What specific action will you take to show your love for Jesus this week by showing love for the poor?

Go with the Word

The Poor

The Gospel in Art by the Peasants of Solentiname is a collection of commentaries by peasants on the gospel passage read at Mass each Sunday. Solentiname is in Nicaragua in Central America. The following commentaries are on John 12:1–8.

Oscar: "If they sold it, it would have gone to only a small number of the poor, and the poor of the world are countless. On the other hand, when she offered it to Jesus, she was giving it, in his person, to all the poor. That made it clear it was Jesus we believe in. And believing in Jesus makes us concerned about other people, and we'll even get to create a society where there'll be no poor. Because if we're Christians, there shouldn't be any poor."

Old Tomas: "There's lots of ways of being poor; a poor person can be somebody with an arm missing . . . or an orphan child, without parents. These will be in the community. There'll always be people like that in need, but of course if we're Christians they won't be poor, in poverty; if they're among us, that is, we won't let them perish."

Ernesto: "I think what he's saying is that he's going away but that in place of him the poor are left. What that woman was doing with him, they'd have to do later with the poor, because he wasn't going to be there any longer, or rather, we were going to have his presence in the poor."

Felipe: "And people like us who don't have perfumes or luxurious things to give because we're poor—we can give other valuable things that we have. We can offer our lives as Jesus did."

Philip and Sally Scharper, eds., *The Gospel in Art by the Peasants of Solentiname* (Maryknoll, N.Y.: Orbis Books, 1984). Used by permission.

Palm Branches and a Cross

Christ humbled Christ's self and became obedient to the point of death—even death on a cross. Therefore God also highly exalted Jesus and gave Jesus the name that is above every name.

Philippians 2:8–9

Bible Reading: Philippians 2:5–11

Additional Bible Readings: Isaiah 50:4–9a
                                 Psalm 118:1–2, 19–29
                                 Luke 19:28–40

Enter the Word

- What emotions does Palm/Passion Sunday evoke in you?
- What does it mean for you, in word and deed, to "confess that Jesus Christ is Savior to the glory of God"?

Holy Week inspires extreme emotions. Palm Sunday is a day of rejoicing and celebrating through church parades, children waving palm branches, and joyous music. Maundy Thursday is bittersweet, mixing the intimacy of communion with the shadow of imminent death. Good Friday is a day of grief and loss. And just when all seems lost, Easter reverses the mood once again.

As you experience Holy Week, be aware of its dramatic realities. Make additional time for prayer each day. Start now by thinking through the events symbolized during the week.

Recall the story of Jesus' triumphal entry into Jerusalem and his crying over that city the same day. Think of the arrest, the trial, and the pain of the Crucifixion itself before Easter.

Read Philippians 2:5–11, which explains why Jesus was willing to experience the events of Holy Week. Isaiah 50:4–9a prophesies the horrendous treatment that God's servant will suffer. Psalm 118:1–2, 19–29 describes the rejection of the "chief cornerstone," which Christians understand to be Christ. And Luke 19:28–40 records the events surrounding Jesus' procession into Jerusalem. The readings for this week challenge us to see that there is a very public side to following Christ. We follow Christ as a community; through the public events of the church during Holy Week, we move as a community with Jesus through his death.

> *Holy One of God, empower me to confess you as Savior and to bear witness to that belief in all arenas of my life. Amen.*

Engage the Word

- How does Christ's humble willingness to submit to death on the cross help the early church to discern its own identity?

What is the path to Easter? Sometimes Protestant worship moves from the rejoicing of Palm Sunday to the rejoicing of Easter without going through the agony of Good Friday. It helps that now Palm Sunday is also recognized as Passion ("suffering") Sunday, for Jesus did ride on to his death.

In his letter to the Philippians, Paul did not forget the Crucifixion. He appealed to the Philippians as a community to show love, compassion, and sympathy and to be of one mind (Philippians 2:1–2). But what is that one mind? It is the mind of Christ. Paul wrote, "Let the same mind be in you that was in Christ Jesus" (v. 5).

Paul introduced what is known as a Christ-hymn (most translations show its poetic form) to the church at Philippi. Apparently it was a hymn already used by early Christians before Paul incorporated it into his letter. For Paul, the hymn showed the mind of Christ.

The hymn may have been intended to contrast Christ and Adam (note Romans 5:14–15 and 1 Corinthians 15:22). Like

Adam ("humanity"), Jesus bore the image or form of God (Genesis 1:26). But unlike Adam (tempted to "be like God"; see Genesis 3:5), Jesus "did not regard equality with God as something to be exploited" (Philippians 2:6). Rather than seeking to exalt himself, he humbly emptied himself as a servant in human form (v. 7), obedient to the point of death (v. 8; Adam was disobedient—see Romans 5:19).

Here Paul broke into the hymn's poetic form and added the words "even death on a cross." Though the world saw the cross as foolishness and weakness, Paul saw it as God's wisdom and power (1 Corinthians 1:18–25), the wisdom and power of God's love (Romans 5:8). It was a love that reached out to heal broken relationships between God and people and among people. This is the mind of Christ—to be a humble servant of God's reconciling love that may lead to "even death on a cross."

"Therefore," the hymn continues, God has exalted him and given him a name that invites all humanity to worship ("every knee should bend," v. 10) and confess that "Jesus Christ is Savior" (an early Christian baptismal confession) to the glory of God (vv. 9–11). The glory does not end in Jesus himself but in God.

This ties in with the reading from Luke: "Blessed is the Sovereign who comes in the name of God!" (Luke 19:38). Jesus as sovereign rode on to die on a cross before he received the crown, the Resurrection.

Paul wanted a community whose mind had been transformed (note Romans 12:2) and whose identity was formed by the mind of Christ to live to the glory of God in the Spirit of love. Jesus as the Christ, the suffering Messiah, is sovereign, the ruler of those who move from Palm Sunday to Easter through Good Friday and "even death on a cross."

Respond to the Word

- How does being a part of a community of faith that confesses Jesus as the Savior strengthen your own faith?
- What will you do this week to walk with Jesus from the palm-strewn road of Jerusalem to the cross at Calvary?

Go with the Word

Blessing of the Palms

O God, who in Jesus Christ
triumphantly entered Jerusalem,
heralding a week of pain and sorrow,
be with us now
as we follow the way of the cross.
In these events of defeat and victory,
you have sealed the closeness
of death and resurrection,
of humiliation and exaltation.
We thank you for these branches
that promise to become for us
symbols of martyrdom and majesty.
Bless them and us
that their use this day may announce in our time
that Christ has come
and that Christ will come again.
Amen! Come, Christ Jesus!

"Blessing of the Palms," in *United Church of Christ Book of Worship*
(New York: United Church of Christ Office of Church Life and
Leadership, 1986), 189. Used by permission.

Paul T. Granlund, *Resurrection II*, cast bronze, 1973, as reproduced in *ARTS Advocate* (UCC Fellowship in the Arts) 12, no. 1 (winter 1990), cover. Used by permission of the artist.

Easter

The difficult journey of Lent is now over. The tears of Good Friday's grief give way to inexpressible joy at dawn on Easter morning as Mary Magdalene discovers that Jesus is alive. The tomb could not contain him, for God prevailed over death. Paul T. Granlund's *Resurrection* captures the moment when the crucified Savior, arms outstretched, emerges triumphant over death. As you focus on Granlund's sculpture, meditate on the impact of Jesus' resurrection on your own life.

Early Christians observed Easter on the day after Passover ended, regardless of the day of the week. Today, Western Christians celebrate Easter on the first Sunday after the first full moon following the vernal equinox. For this reason, Easter is not a constant date, but falls on a Sunday between March 22 and April 25. The season itself extends for fifty days through the festival of Pentecost.

White is the liturgical color for the Great Fifty Days, as Easter and the season following is sometimes known. Baptisms and initiations into the church, such as confirmation, are often celebrated during this festive season. On Pentecost Sunday, red reminds the church of the tongues of fire through which God's Spirit was poured out upon the disciples so that God's works of power could be proclaimed to all in their own languages.

Weep No More

Jesus said to Mary Magdalene, "Woman, why are you weeping? Whom are you looking for?" Supposing Jesus to be the gardener, she answered, "Sir, if you have carried Jesus away, tell me where you have laid him, and I will take him away." Jesus said to her, "Mary!" She turned and responded in Hebrew, "Rabbouni!" (which means Teacher).

John 20:15–16

Bible Reading:	John 20:1–18
Additional Bible Readings:	Acts 10:34–43
	Isaiah 65:17–25
	Psalm 118:1–2, 14–24
	1 Corinthians 15:19–26
	Luke 24:1–12

Enter the Word

- What emotions do you experience when a loved one dies?
- How might you feel in the presence of the risen Christ?

Set an unlit candle before you. Read John 20:1–18 silently.

Imagine it is Easter morning before dawn. You are alone in a garden. Feel the dampness in the air and at your feet. Smell the earth, the flowers and grass, the fresh morning air. Meditate on your reasons for coming to the garden.

Then light the candle and read John 20:1–18, this time aloud. Focus on the candle flame. Imagine that in the garden you see a light. Envision yourself moving toward the light. Experience fear, excitement, or whatever other emotions you may have. Think about what you expect to happen during this garden visit.

Hear Jesus calling your name. Imagine your response.

Read Luke's account of Easter morning as found in Luke 24:1–12 and compare it to John's record. Continue your reflection by reading Isaiah 65:17–25, which tells of a new heaven and a new earth. Ponder how Jesus' resurrection begins to bring forth this new heaven and earth.

Read Psalm 118:1–2, 14–24 and imagine yourself still standing in the opening to the empty tomb; see the bright light of the angels—"it is marvelous in our eyes" (v. 23); hear the words of praise and worship, "This is the day that God has made; let us rejoice and be glad in it" (v. 24).

In 1 Corinthians 15:19–26 Paul explains the significance of the Resurrection. As you read Acts 10:34–43, note that Jesus' saving work is not for a select few but is available to all.

> *Risen Christ, I stand in awe as I hear you call my name.*
> *Empower me to respond to your saving grace. Amen.*

Engage the Word

- How would John's story have helped the early church deal with Jesus' death and resurrection?

The story in the Gospel of John of Mary Magdalene at the tomb on Easter morning moves dramatically from her expectation of finding the body of Jesus to her encounter with the risen Christ. Out of that experience, she became the first person in this Gospel to proclaim the Resurrection, "I have seen the Savior" (v. 18).

She appears in this gospel only twice: at the cross with other women (John 19:25) and at the tomb alone. The tomb story in John 20 tells three times of her weeping over the missing body of Jesus (vv. 11, 13, 15). Then the risen Jesus called her name, would not let her fit him into old ways of knowing him, and commissioned her to go and tell.

When she first came to the tomb and saw that the stone had been removed, she ran to tell Peter and "the other disciple" (v. 2, the beloved disciple whom the Gospel of John never names). She could tell them only that Jesus was missing from the tomb (v. 2). The two race to the tomb, the other disciple winning the race. Each has a look. Peter simply "saw" (v. 6) but the other disciple "saw and believed" (v. 8). It is not clear what he believed, "for as yet they did not understand the scripture, that he must rise from the dead" (v. 9). The two simply "returned to their homes" (v. 10).

"But Mary stood weeping outside the tomb" (v. 11). She wept to the angels (v. 13). She wept to Jesus, mistaking him for the gardener (v. 15). The first words of the risen Jesus were words to Mary, "Woman, why are you weeping? Whom are you looking for?" For the third time in the story Mary spoke of Jesus' missing body (vv. 2, 13, 15).

But when Jesus called her name, "Mary," she turned and, at last recognizing him, said "Rabbouni" (v. 16). His calling her name created recognition, response, and a new relationship. It recalls Jesus' earlier words in John: "He calls his own sheep by name" (John 10:3).

The risen Jesus was no longer simply the Jesus whom Mary had known earlier. She could not hold on to or control the risen Christ. Once ascended to be with God, Christ could be known to her through the presence of the Holy Spirit (see John 14:16–18, 23).

Now the risen Christ sends her to go and tell the disciples of the ascension and their new relationship with God. She does so and declares, "I have seen Jesus" (vv. 17–18).

Earlier she ran to tell Peter and the other disciple of what she thought was a dead Jesus, taken from the tomb (v. 2). Now she could tell of the risen Christ. Now she would weep no more. Now (in the words from the Isaiah reading) "no more shall the sound of weeping be heard" (Isaiah 65:19).

Respond to the Word

- What response does the empty tomb evoke in you?
- To whom can you tell the good news that Jesus is risen? How will you do that this week?

Go with the Word

Resurrection

Look at the sculpture *Resurrection*, found on the divider for Easter (p. 146).

Art representing the Crucifixion and the risen Christ is commonly seen, but art which attempts to present the moment of resurrection is rare. In this representation Paul Granlund has attempted to interpret that moment. The figure of Christ is shown bent over, knees and head nearly touching. The arms are outstretched in a position of crucifixion. The figure is bound on three sides by slabs of the tomb and on the fourth by the earth.

The movement of the body is not downward, but upward and out. The outstretching of the arms and the propelling tension in the legs emphasize the surging strength of this Christ as the lid of the tomb is thrown off. The walls of death are not strong enough to prevail against the power of God. Almost birdlike, this figure is breaking free of earth's gravity, no longer under the sway of ordinary time and space.

This is the power of resurrection. Ponder the power of Christ's resurrection and its effect on humanity.

Peace Be with You

When it was evening on that day, the first day of the week, and the doors of the house where the disciples had met were locked for fear of the religious authorities, Jesus came and stood among them and said, "Peace be with you."

John 20:19

Bible Reading:	John 20:19–31
Additional Bible Readings:	Acts 5:27–32 Psalm 118:14–29 or Psalm 150 Revelation 1:4–8

Enter the Word

- How do you define "peace"?
- In what areas of your life do you need to experience peace?

Find a quiet place and a time to be alone. Sit in a comfortable position and take several deep breaths, allowing yourself to become calm and relaxed. Through silent prayer, either with or without words, ask God to be with you.

Focus on the word "peace" and what it means to you. Identify places where peace exists in your life and give thanks. Also identify places where there is "un-peace" and ask God to heal you of whatever is disrupting peace in your life.

Now read John 20:19–31 aloud. Picture the upper room where the disciples gathered on the evening of the first Easter. Imagine yourself as one of the disciples. See yourself entering the room, locking the door for fear of the Jewish leaders who plotted Jesus' death. Look around you. See the faces of Peter, James, John, and Andrew. Be aware of your thoughts and feelings. See Jesus enter the room. Look at his face. Be open to experience him in a new, life transforming way.

Return to your thoughts about peace and "un-peace" in your own life. Tell Jesus about one of the areas of "un-peace." Sit quietly and listen for his answer.

Read Acts 5:27–32 and contemplate the peace of Christ that must have existed within Peter as he dared to give his witness before the Jewish council. Psalm 118:14–29 gives thanks for God's deliverance. Psalm 150 is a glorious hymn of praise to God, who has done mighty deeds. Revelation 1:4–8 introduces the letters to the seven churches in western Asia Minor.

> *Let the peace of God which surpasses all understanding keep my heart and my mind in Christ Jesus. Amen.*

Engage the Word

- How does the story of the risen Christ's encounters with the disciples, especially Thomas, help John's community to believe in Christ and experience God's peace?

Peace is often seen as the absence of war. But in the Bible, peace (*eirene* in the Greek), with its rich background in the Hebrew *shalom*, is much more than the absence of war. It is the presence of wholeness and health, harmony and security, justice and truth, relationships that are intact with God, with others, with the earth.

In last Sunday's reading from John's Gospel, the risen Jesus appeared to Mary Magdalene. In this Sunday's reading he appeared to his disciples on Easter evening without Thomas, and then again a week later with Thomas. Three times he said to them, "Peace be with you" (vv. 19, 21, 26). His word of peace had comforted and encouraged them before his death (John 14:27, 16:33).

Now the disciples needed to hear it even more. As Jesus faced death, they all scattered and left him alone (John 16:32). They were fearful and broken: fearful that what happened to him might happen to them, broken in their relationship with him. They had deserted him; he did not desert them. He came to them to reestablish his relationship with them, to let them rejoice that he was alive, and to make their broken lives whole again.

But Jesus not only renewed his relationship with them; he trusted them with his mission of love (John 20:21). He breathed new life into them (note Genesis 2:7) and empowered them with the Holy Spirit (v. 22). Just as his work was to take away the sin of the world (the breaking of relationship with God, see John 1:29), now they had the task of forgiving ("letting go") peoples' sins and not retaining ("holding onto") them (v. 23). He "ordained" his followers to be bringers of peace and new relationships as he was.

Thomas was not there. Earlier he had shown some courage (John 11:16); he even disrupted Jesus' word and asked him a question (John 14:4–5). Now he refused to believe the other disciples' words until he had seen and touched (v. 25). That chance came a week later. Jesus invited him to touch, to "not doubt but believe" (v. 27). Thomas confessed, "My Lord and my God" (v. 28).

Thomas belonged to those disciples who knew Jesus as a tangible person. The writer of John's Gospel and his community some sixty years later did not. Therefore, Jesus' final words to Thomas packed much meaning for them: "Have you believed because you have seen me? Blessed are those who have not seen and yet have come to believe" (v. 29).

Today's believers are in the same position as John's community: called to believe without seeing and to enter into relationship with the risen Christ. Christians cannot prove and explain Jesus' resurrection. But the Resurrection explains their existence as Christians and enables them to forgive and say, "Peace be with you."

Respond to the Word

- How can you, working together with others, help to bring peace to a group that is troubled?
- To whom can you offer Christ's peace this week? How will you do that?

Go with the Word

Heal Me, Hands of Jesus

Heal me, hands of Jesus,
and search out all my pain;
restore my hope, remove my fear,
and bring me peace again.

Cleanse me, blood of Jesus,
take bitterness away;
let me forgive as one forgiven
and bring me peace today.

Know me, mind of Jesus,
and show me all my sin;
dispel the memories of guilt
and bring me peace within.

Fill me, joy of Jesus,
anxiety shall cease,
and heaven's serenity be mine,
for Jesus brings me peace.

Come, Have Breakfast

When they had gone ashore, they saw a charcoal fire there, with fish on it, and bread. Jesus said to them, "Bring some of the fish that you have just caught." So Simon Peter went aboard and hauled the net ashore, full of large fish, a hundred fifty-three of them; and though there were so many, the net was not torn. Jesus said to them, "Come and have breakfast."

John 21:9–12a

Bible Reading: John 21:1–19

Additional Bible Readings: Acts 9:1–6 (7–20)
                                    Psalm 30
                                    Revelation 5:11–14

Enter the Word

- What might it be like to be Jesus' guest for breakfast?
- How does Jesus invite you, fill you, and send you out to serve?

Find a quiet place to sit comfortably, perhaps taking a beverage or snack with you. Imagine yourself with the disciples sitting by the sea. Jesus has appeared to you. After a week full of death and despair, new life and promise fills your thoughts, exhausts you, and brings you to this familiar place.

Read John 21:1–19. Imagine you are Peter. Experience the frustration and other emotions you had as you fished through the night, catching nothing. Think about your response to the stranger who appeared. Imagine your amazement when you saw the miraculous catch of fish. Say whatever comes to mind when you realize that this stranger is Jesus.

Think of times when you have received spiritual food. Perhaps you have felt nourished from the personal study of Scripture or from a group Bible study. Maybe you have been fed spiritually by the words or actions of another person or by a group where there was a strong sense of community. Music, art, or drama may have helped you feel the presence of God. Or perhaps you have felt strengthened and sustained by the very people you reached out to help. List some of the ways that you have received spiritual nourishment.

Receive nourishment from God's Word by studying today's additional readings. Acts 9:1–6 (7–20) tells the familiar story of Saul's transforming encounter with Christ on the road to Damascus. In Psalm 30 the psalmist gives thanks to God for healing. Revelation 5:11–14 is also a song of praise to the slain Lamb, the risen Christ.

> In this quiet moment I ask you to feed me, Jesus, with the life-sustaining food that nourishes my soul. Amen.

Engage the Word

- How might this story of Jesus sharing a meal with his disciples have inspired John's community?

During Jesus' ministry, he fed his followers along with the multitude (John 6:1–13) and fed them again at the Last Supper (John 13:1–38). In John 21:1–19, Jesus feeds them as their risen Savior.

This passage from John tells of another appearance of the risen Jesus to the disciples. His other resurrection appearances were all in Jerusalem. This one is back in the disciples' home region of Galilee. Surprisingly, the story assumes that after the disciples' two experiences of the risen Jesus in Jerusalem (John 20:19–29), they just went home to Galilee to go fishing. (Many scholars see chapter 21 as an epilogue to chapters 1–20 with John 20 as the original end of this gospel.)

As a fishing story it bears a resemblance to another (Luke 5:1–11). In both stories they fished all night and caught nothing. In both, it is obedience to Jesus' words that brought results (John 21:6; Luke 5:5–6). In John, they did not at first recognize that it was Jesus who spoke to them (vv. 4–5). It was after the big catch that the "beloved disciple" said, "It is the Lord," and Peter and the others head for Jesus on the shore (vv. 7–8).

In John, Jesus called for some fish. Peter hauled in one hundred fifty-three with no tear in the net (v. 11, scholars have fun trying to figure out the symbolism here: it does seem to point to a united community in an overwhelming mission of "catching people," note Luke 5:10).

Jesus then said, "Come and have breakfast. . . . Jesus came and took the bread and gave it to them, and did the same with the fish" (vv. 12, 13). Christians have long connected this story to the Holy Communion. There the risen Christ feeds his followers again and again.

Why did he feed the disciples? The story about Peter that follows (vv. 15–17) suggests a reason. Jesus fed Peter and the others so that they in turn could feed and tend Jesus' lambs and sheep and carry on his mission (note John 10:16). Peter denied Jesus three times. Now Jesus called for his love three times, a love that means caring for others.

Jesus promised no rose garden. The reading points rather to Peter's death by crucifixion (vv. 18–19). Tradition has it that he died in Rome crucified upside down. This is where Jesus' command to "Follow me" (v. 19) led Peter.

"Come and have breakfast" has such a happy ring about it, and it may be a joyful time at Jesus' table. But it also has the overtone, "Come and die." That bold invitation is spoken to those who follow Jesus and feed his sheep in the midst of wolves and thieves and bandits (see John 10:7–15).

Respond to the Word

- How can you work with others to provide food for those whose nets are empty?
- What can you do this week to offer the Bread of Life to someone who does not know Jesus?

Go with the Word

They Found God

*They met Him again after
they had seen Him killed.
And then after they
had been formed into
a little society or community,
they found God somehow
inside them as well,
directing them,
making them able to do things
they could not do before.*

C. S. Lewis, *Mere Christianity* (New York: Macmillan Company, 1952), 127.

Shepherd Psalm

God is my shepherd, I shall not want.

Psalm 23:1

Bible Reading:	Psalm 23
Additional Bible Readings:	Acts 9:36–43
	Revelation 7:9–17
	John 10:22–30

Enter the Word

- Why, when all else seems lost, do you think that Psalm 23 and the image of the good shepherd is remembered by many people?
- How has Psalm 23 sustained you in a difficult time?

Begin your study time by reflecting on your memories of Psalm 23. Recall when you first heard or learned the psalm. Perhaps you memorized it as a child in church school. Or you may have challenged yourself to memorize it after hearing it in congregational worship or at a funeral service. Perhaps a favorite relative said it to you when as a child you rested in her or his arms. Remember when you first recognized the special meaning this psalm holds for many people.

Say or write as much of Psalm 23 as you can from memory. Even if you cannot remember the exact wording, recall as many of the images and phrases as you can in random order. Then read Psalm 23 aloud from your Bible. Imagine yourself as the one being led beside peaceful waters. See yourself in the valley of crisis or death and feel the shepherd's loving care.

Try writing this psalm in your own words. Use images and ideas that are familiar to you to express the potent message of the psalmist. Or you may find it helpful to try a technique called reverse paraphrase. Here you write the *opposite* of what the psalm says. Such an exercise helps you see just how important God the Good Shepherd is in your life.

Continue your study by reading the verses from Revelation 7:9–17, which remind us that the Lamb of God is also the Shepherd who "will wipe away every tear from their eyes" (v. 17). Also read Acts 9:36–43, which shows Peter, whom Christ had called to feed his lambs, raising up Dorcas from the dead. Look also at John 10:22–30 in which Jesus announces that he is the shepherd who gives eternal life.

> *I thank you, my Shepherd, for I rest secure within your sheepfold even when life's crises seek to devour me. Amen.*

Engage the Word

- How might the image of the shepherd have helped the people of the psalmist's day and later communities of Christians to experience God's love for them?

The Bible has many images for God. In rural settings where sheep were common, a major image was God as shepherd. New Testament writers transferred this image to Jesus. In the reading from John, Jesus as the good shepherd says, "My sheep hear my voice. I know them, and they follow me" (John 10:27). In the reading from Revelation, Jesus as the Lamb "will be their shepherd, and he will guide them to springs of the water of life" (Revelation 7:17).

For many people, Psalm 23 is the most familiar of the psalms. More people know it by heart than any other. Often it is read at the bedside of the sick and at funerals. Even though many people no longer have much direct contact with agricultural images, God as shepherd still touches many with comfort and hope.

The psalm is attributed to King David, once a shepherd himself. It may first have been a psalm for a king to confess at his coronation. Some of its symbols are more royal or religious than pastoral: table, anointing with oil, cup, house of God. These are combined with pastoral symbols: green pastures, still waters, right paths, rod and staff. David himself was a real shepherd, a king, and a religious man. If he composed it, it is not surprising that he should combine these various symbols.

God once spoke to David, "You . . . shall be shepherd of my people Israel" (2 Samuel 5:2). But Psalm 23 confesses that God is the true shepherd. All other shepherds are subordinate to God. In fact, human shepherds (political and religious leaders) often are unfaithful. Ezekiel 34 is a great shepherd chapter. Given unfaithful shepherds/leaders, God takes over as shepherd (read especially the very moving vv. 11–17).

Psalm 23 is very realistic about life. On the one hand are the beautiful, positive images, both royal/religious and pastoral (noted above). On the other, there are the shadowy valley (or valley of the shadow of death), evil (v. 4), and enemies (v. 5).

To know God as shepherd does not mean escape from the harsh realities of life. But it does mean that God restores life and leads in right paths in God's right-making purpose (v. 3). It does mean that evil can be confronted without fear (v. 4). It does mean that God anoints and prepares a table (v. 5; Christians might think of these images and relate them to baptism and the communion table). It does mean that, throughout all of life, God's goodness and mercy are present for celebration with others in the sheepfold of God's house (v. 6).

At a church program a little boy was to say by heart, "The Lord is my shepherd, I shall not want." He started, "The Lord is my shepherd." Then, forgetting the rest, he stopped. This happened three times. Finally he said confidently, "The Lord is my shepherd, what more do I want?"

Respond to the Word

- How can a group you belong to provide security and comfort for others who need such pastoral care?
- What shepherding care do you need from God this week?

Go with the Word

A Shepherd

You watch over your creation,
a shepherd
with whom all living things are safe.
You know us all
and keep us
wherever we move.
O God, do this,
we ask you
all the days of our lives—
may we never want
and may we enter your rest
and know your peace.
Today and every day
of our lives.

Huub Oosterhuis, *Your Word Is Near: Contemporary Christian Prayers,* trans. N. D. Smith (New York: Paulist Press, 1968), 23. Used by permission.

All Things New

Then I saw a new heaven and a new earth; for the first heaven and the first earth had passed away, and the sea was no more. And I heard a loud voice from the throne saying, "See, the home of God is among mortals. God will dwell with them as their God; and they will be God's peoples, and God will indeed be with them and will wipe every tear from their eyes. Death will be no more; mourning and crying and pain will be no more, for the first things have passed away." And the one who was seated on the throne said, "See, I am making all things new."

Revelation 21:1, 3–5a

Bible Reading:	Revelation 21:1–6
Additional Bible Readings:	Acts 11:1–18
	Psalm 148
	John 13:31–35

Enter the Word

- What kinds of responses do people have to new situations?
- What would you like to be new in your life right now?

Sit quietly and think about the words "new" and "newness." Reflect on new dimensions in your own life right now. Perhaps you have a new interest or a new friend. Maybe you are reading something that is challenging your thinking. Possibly you are making an effort to change some old habits. Ponder ways that newness of thought, lifestyle, or hope might enrich you.

Reflect on your community. Compare it to God's vision of life where love and justice prevail. Think about how your community is exercising stewardship over God's earth. Name ways in which you wish this community could be "made new."

Read Revelation 21:1–6 and think about how you would envision a new heaven and earth. Then read Acts 11:1–18, which describes how God's Holy Spirit brought transforming newness to a Gentile community. Psalm 148 calls upon all of God's creation to sing praise. John 13:31–35 records the new commandment that Jesus gave the disciples—love one another.

> *Transform me, O God, so that I may experience the newness of life offered to me in Christ Jesus. Amen.*

Engage the Word

- How would the Revelation to John have helped persecuted Christians hold fast to their faith?

The Revelation to John probably was written during the reign of the Emperor Domitian and his persecution of Christians in the 90s of the first century. Domitian wanted to be worshiped as God. He tried to compel persons to do this by putting incense on the altar for use in emperor worship. The Revelation to John challenged such idolatry and served as "a call for the endurance and faith of the saints" (Revelation 13:10; see also 14:12; "saints" are Christians). Revelation 21:1–6 lifts up a vision of God's new world for those who are faithful in the midst of persecution (the entire vision is described in Revelation 21:1–22:5).

A crucial question that John sought to answer is, "Who is in charge of history?" Is it the Roman emperor? No, it is God, "the Alpha and the Omega [the first and last letters of the Greek alphabet], the beginning and the end" (Revelation 21:6; see also 1:8). To worship the emperor might result in a short-term gain, but its ultimate result would be eternal loss. The final conqueror will not be the emperor but God Almighty.

This kind of writing is called apocalyptic, or revelatory. It has its roots in Jewish writings that revealed hope for the future in the midst of tough times. With background in the Hebrew Scriptures (see Isaiah 65:17; 66:22), John pointed to "a new heaven and a new earth" (v. 1). With Jerusalem as the center of new hope (see Isaiah 65:19–20), John wrote of the new Jerusalem, "coming down out of heaven from God" (note v. 10; 3:12) with the joyous marriage image of an adorned bride (note Isaiah 61:10).

The vision is not one of earth lifted up to heaven, but of heaven come down to transform earth and human life with the presence of God. "The home of God is among mortals" (v. 3).

In a setting of persecution and mourning and death, John envisioned that God "will wipe every tear from their eyes. Death will be no more; mourning and crying and pain will be no more" (v. 4; note also 7:17; Isaiah 25:8; 35:10). To the thirsty, God "will give water as a gift from the spring of the water of life" (v. 6; note also 7:17; 22:1, 17). The God who sits on the throne as the Alpha and the Omega and ruler of the world proclaims, "See, I am making all things new" (v. 5; see Isaiah 42:9; 43:19).

John's vision was intended to encourage the churches of his time (note Revelation 1:11) and to call for faithful living in the midst of political persecution. His vision forever challenged the worship of any nation that exalts itself.

Hope for the future does not lie in putting trust in any "emperor" but in the Alpha and the Omega. God will not only dwell with people in the future but already has come to meet death and mourning, crying and pain, in the death and resurrection of the Lamb (note Revelation 21:22–23, 22:1, 3). Christians not only envision a new future; they seek to live that death-defying vision now as followers of the Lamb.

Respond to the Word

- What steps can you take with others to live this "death-defying vision" as witnesses on behalf of the Lamb?
- How will John's vision of newness empower you this week?

Go with the Word

Making New; That's What's Going On

Now, do you want to know a secret? *Making new; that's what's going on in the world;* that's what's happening. The Holy City is not future perfect, it's present tense. (Check out the Greek verbs in the text!) Now the Holy City is descending. Now God is making things new. Right now God is wiping tears and easing pain and overcoming the power of death in the world.

Now! There's nothing otherworldly about the vision; it's happening now in the midst of our worn, torn, broken world. And with the eyes of faith, you can see it happening.

David G. Buttrick, in Cornish R. Rogers and Joseph R. Jeter, eds.,
Preaching through the Apocalypse: Sermons from Revelation (St. Louis:
Chalice Press, 1992), 162.

Open Heart, Open Home

A certain woman named Lydia, a worshiper of God, was listening to us; she was from the city of Thyatira and a dealer in purple cloth. God opened her heart to listen eagerly to what was said by Paul. When she and her household were baptized, she urged us, saying, "If you have judged me to be faithful to the Sovereign, come and stay at my home." And she prevailed upon us.

Acts 16:14–15

Bible Reading: Acts 16:9–15

Additional Bible Readings: Psalm 67
Revelation 21:10, 21:22–22:5
John 14:23–29 or John 5:1–9

Enter the Word

- What words or actions make people feel welcomed?
- How do you show hospitality to others?

Read Acts 16:9–15 to yourself. Then close your eyes and try to feel what Paul, an itinerant stranger, felt as he arrived in Philippi. Imagine his fears, his frustrations, his longings for the mundane, simple comforts of home.

Reread verses 9–13, the point at which Paul goes to the place of prayer and finds a gathering of women there. Imagine how Paul felt and what he might have said.

Continue reading the story. Let Lydia become vivid in your imagination. She sold purple cloth. She worshiped God. She was the head of her household and a businesswoman in an age and culture of few businesswomen. Imagine her height and stature, her weight, her eyes, her smile. Imagine the shape and touch of her hands. Let the story speak to you. Lydia listened to Paul (v. 14). His words were life-changing, for "she and her household were baptized (v. 15). Then she invited Paul and his companions to her home, prevailing upon them to accept.

Close your eyes and recall those people who have prevailed upon you and welcomed you into their hearts and home. Remember times when you invited others to accept your hospitality.

Reading Psalm 67, a song of thanksgiving for a good harvest. Revelation 21:10, 21:22—22:5, mentioned in last week's study, speaks of our home Jerusalem as it will be when the new heaven and new earth appear. John 14:23–29 reminds us that God's Word is our home. In John 5:1–9, Jesus heals a man who had been paralyzed, giving him the chance to feel at home in his own body.

Help me to open my heart and home to you, O God. Amen.

Engage the Word

- What effect might the story of Paul's missionary work have had on Luke's community?

The Acts of the Apostles really might be better named the Acts of the Holy Spirit. It is Luke's story of the spread of the good news throughout the eastern Mediterranean world from Jerusalem to Rome by persons empowered by the Spirit. That spread moved across the barriers of nation and language, gender and race, religion and social class, to bring "good news of great joy to all the people" (Luke 2:10).

In Acts, Luke looked back several decades to tell of this earlier missionary expansion. He wanted to inspire his own community for their mission and create a favorable climate for that mission to continue "with all boldness and without hindrance" (Acts 28:31).

In Luke's story in Acts, the two central persons are Peter and Paul, but in chapters 13 to 28 Paul is the main bearer of the good news in the power of the Spirit. The Spirit led Paul and his companions, guiding them in both where to go and where not to go. In the verses preceding today's reading, the Spirit forbade them to go to Asia (Acts 16:6–8).

In Acts 16:9–10, a vision led Paul and his companions to turn their mission westward to Macedonia (a Roman province in northern Greece). In the vision a person called out, "Come over to Macedonia and help us." And so they sailed from city to city until they came to Philippi, a leading city in Macedonia (vv. 11–12). Paul's ministry led to the founding of a church, to which he later wrote his letter to the Philippians.

With his strong concern for the partnership of women and men in ministry, Luke's story lifts up the businesswoman Lydia. In a Sabbath context of speaking and praying, Lydia (already one who worshiped God) listened to Paul and his friends and "opened her heart" (v. 14) to the message Paul proclaimed. That message was God's good news of Jesus with its call to repentance and forgiveness of sins (see Luke 24:46–47).

Following a typical pattern in Acts, after receiving the Word, Lydia and her household were baptized. But her new faith didn't stop with her relationship to God's good news in Jesus. It led to her opening her home to Paul and his friends. A sign of her faithfulness to God was hospitality to others. One might say that her vertical relationship of faith in God expressed itself in her horizontal relationship of love for others (note Acts 16:40).

In the reading from John, Jesus said, "Those who love me will keep my word, and my Father will love them, and we will come to them and make our home with them" (John 14:23). For Lydia to open her heart meant love and hospitality for both God and Jesus, as well as Paul and his companions. Open hearts lead to open homes.

Respond to the Word

- Read the excerpt from *Come Home!* What can you do this week to help others feel more at home in the church?
- What steps can you take to make yourself more at home wherever you go?

Go with the Word

Home

First and foremost, I felt a sense of being home, a place where "they have to take you in," but also, a place where they *want* to take you in. In the ideal experience of it, home is a place for healing wounds and celebrating fulfillment. It's an environment which welcomes you to kick off your shoes, sink into an armchair, and put your feet up. You can be yourself. The masks are down, and you become as comfortable and vulnerable as a sleepy puppy. How I wished the church could be such a place for me!

Chris Glaser, *Come Home!* (San Francisco: HarperCollins, 1990), xii.

Connections

**One day, as we were going to the place of prayer, we met
a slave girl who had a spirit of divination and brought her
owners a great deal of money by fortune-telling. But
when her owners saw that their hope of making money
was gone, they seized Paul and Silas and dragged them
into the marketplace before the authorities.**

Acts 16:16, 19

Bible Reading:	Acts 16:16–34
Additional Bible Readings:	Psalm 97
	Revelation 22:12–14, 16–17, 20–21
	John 17:20–26

Enter the Word

- How does faith connect a person to God?
- What connections do you make between your faith and
  money, politics, power, or salvation?

Quickly read Acts 16:16–34. Without looking back at the text,
tell the story in your own words. Read the story again, looking for
details that you missed in your telling of it.

On a sheet of paper draw a vertical line down the center. Title
the left column "Misuse of Power" and the right, "Constructive Use
of Power." Again read Acts 16:16–34, this time jotting down ways
you see power misused and ways you see it used constructively.

Look for a relationship between the drive for money and the misuse of power. Try to identify connections among faith, power, and money.

Consider how your own actions, including your uses of power and money, are connected to your faith. Ponder the ways in which your faith is a catalyst and guide for your actions. Focus on an incident or two that shows these connections. Read the additional scriptures and try to connect them to the passage from Acts.

> Gracious God, help me connect my beliefs with my actions so that others may experience your loving salvation. Amen.

Engage the Word

- What connections might Luke's first readers have drawn between this story and the relationship between their personal faith and public actions?

Acts 16:16–34 follows immediately the reading for Easter 6. Its setting also is Philippi where Paul met Lydia. The final scene of this story is found in verses 35–40.

No text in the New Testament better combines what might be called personal faith and public action, the internal life of the Christian community and its external witness in the life of the world. It proclaims well that there can be no dichotomy between the personal and social gospel.

On the one hand, there is liberation of a slave girl from personal and economic bondage, persecution of her liberators, the collusion of economic, political, and police power in resisting liberation, and the calling of public officials to accountability. On the other hand, there is praying and singing, speaking the word, washing wounds, baptizing, eating, and rejoicing.

In Luke/Acts, a strong emphasis is placed on prayer in the experiences of both Jesus and the early church. Acts 16:16–34 begins with Paul and his fellow travelers going to a place of prayer day after day. Every day they pass a poor, crying young woman (it recalls the bypassing priest and Levite in Jesus' parable of the compassionate Samaritan), until finally, sufficiently annoyed, Paul frees her in the name of Jesus Christ from her "spirit of divination" (v. 16).

Yet, even in her enslaved condition, she had recognized Paul and his friends' saving message. Her persistent unwillingness to keep silent was the basis for all that followed. Just as Luke lifted up Lydia in the scripture for Easter 6, here he lifts up the girl.

Her owners' realization of their loss of financial gain led to their collusion with city officials, the crowd, and the police to strip, beat, and jail Paul and Silas. Yet in jail these two prisoners sang and prayed. There followed a liberating earthquake (possibly God's response to penal injustice). The jailer, believing that the prisoners would try to escape, was ready to kill himself. But the prisoners had remained in jail.

Then begins the story of the jailer's salvation, including all that accompanies the life of a Christian community: believing in Jesus, speaking, caring, baptizing, eating, and rejoicing, along with the earlier praying and singing. But all of that happened because of a public act that freed a slave girl and landed her liberators in jail.

After the "house church" experience, more public action followed (vv. 35–39). The officials, finally discovering that Paul was a Roman citizen, wanted to quietly sweep the whole event under the rug. But Paul would not let them. He demanded their public accountability. So the story has a certain rhythm that moves from public action to personal faith and back to public action.

This whole story came about because the slave girl would not be silent. She saw in Paul and his friends those who as slaves of the Most High God proclaimed salvation. Finally, she too was freed in the name of Jesus Christ.

Respond to the Word

- Try to identify workers in your community who are exploited. What can you and others do to end this injustice?
- Look through your checkbook, credit card statements, and other financial records. Does your use of money reflect your faith? If not, what change will you make this week?

Go with the Word

Connections

Our knowledge of God *is* in and through each other. Our knowledge of each other *is* in and through God. We act together and find our good in each other and in God, and our power grows together, or we deny our relation and reproduce a violent world where no one experiences holy power.

Beverly Wildung Harrison, *Making Connections: Essays in Feminist Social Ethics*, ed. Carol S. Robb (Boston: Beacon Press, 1985), 41.

Unknown artist, *Pentecost,* World Council of Churches, Indonesian Room, Geneva (World Council of Churches Photography). Photo Oikoumene Archives. Used by permission.

Pentecost

In response to the wooing of God's Spirit on Pentecost, three thousand individuals chose to make a commitment, just as God has invited you to do. Animated and energized by God's Spirit, they each embarked upon a faith journey. But their journey was not to be a solo voyage. They also made a collective commitment to grow toward spiritual maturity by learning, praying, sharing their possessions, breaking bread, fellowshipping, and praising God together. These first believers who comprised the church were one in the Spirit and one in God, just as you and your community of faith are called to be. As you look at *Pentecost* by an unknown artist from Indonesia, imagine yourself as a transformed, empowered member of this community and consider what you would do individually and with the group to live out the Christian life.

During this ordinary time in the weeks between Pentecost and the beginning of Advent, the church focuses on teaching individual members and the gathered community to become the whole people of God. The scripture lessons focus on the stories and teachings of Jesus, as well as other important biblical events that shape Christian identity. Green, the color of growth, adorns the church in this lengthy season.

Pentecost's Many Voices

When the day of Pentecost had come, all were together in one place. And suddenly from heaven there came a sound like the rush of a violent wind, and it filled the entire house where they were sitting. All of them were filled with the Holy Spirit and began to speak in other languages, as the Spirit gave them ability.

Acts 2:1–2, 4

Bible Reading: Acts 2:1–21

Additional Bible Readings: Genesis 11:1–9
Psalm 104:24–34, 35b
Romans 8:14–17
John 14:8–17, 25–27

Enter the Word

- How does the Holy Spirit empower witness for God?
- What relevance does the Pentecost story have for you?

Relax in a comfortable setting and repeat the words "Come, Holy Spirit, come" several times. Think about your image of the Holy Spirit and the thoughts that come to mind when you pray those words. Ponder what the Holy Spirit means to you. Recall times when you know the Spirit acted in your life.

Read aloud the dramatic account of Pentecost from Acts

2:1–21. Imagine yourself as one of the disciples upon whom a tongue of fire rested. Think about your own response to this amazing event, as well as the response of the crowd to your proclamation of God's mighty deeds.

Read the account again, this time experiencing the presence of the Spirit. Feel the rush of wind and the tongue of flame. Hear the diverse languages. Imagine how the many voices of Pentecost might move and shake you this day. Consider how your life might be different if you allowed the Spirit to empower you.

Read today's additional scriptures and try to make connections between them and the Pentecost story recorded in Acts.

> *Come, Holy Spirit. Fill my heart and loose my tongue that I might proclaim your amazing deeds. Amen.*

Engage the Word

- How might Luke's telling of the Pentecost story empower his own Gentile community of faith to witness?

Among New Testament writers, Luke alone tells of the empowering of Jesus' followers with the Holy Spirit at Pentecost. This Jewish harvest festival, also called the Feast of Weeks, came fifty (*pente*) days after Passover and also celebrated the giving of the law to Moses. In Luke's words, Jews had gathered in Jerusalem "from every nation under heaven" (Acts 2:5) for the celebration.

For Luke, this provided the right setting for the Spirit to empower the first preaching of a message that was to reach all peoples across the barriers of all nations and languages. Jesus had instructed his disciples to wait in Jerusalem for such empowering for their mission (Luke 24:49; Acts 1:4–5, 8).

The empowering of the church at Pentecost in Acts parallels the empowering of Jesus at his baptism (Luke 3:21–22). It fulfilled the promise of both John the Baptist and Jesus of Christians' baptism with the Holy Spirit (Luke 3:16; Acts 1:5).

The Spirit empowered Jesus to preach in Nazareth (Luke 4:18–19) and Peter to preach in Jerusalem at Pentecost. It would empower Jesus through his entire ministry from Nazareth to Jerusalem and the early Christians through their entire ministry from Jerusalem to Rome. For Luke, as for some of the prophets, Jerusalem was the place to begin the spread of a message that would reach all nations (see Isaiah 2:2–4; Micah 4:1–4).

As often in the Hebrew heritage, the Pentecost story is both aural and visual, violent wind and purifying fire. The original Greek word for wind, *pneuma*, can be translated also as spirit or breath. The wind points to God's creating spirit or life-giving breath (note Genesis 1:2, 2:7). Now that spirit, God's Holy Spirit, was to burn in Jesus' followers and energize them for their task.

This task involved proclaiming the message about Jesus to all the world. That was Luke's purpose in telling of speaking in tongues. This was not ecstatic speech beyond human language. It was the gift of speaking in the known languages of people from the many different countries Luke listed. They were all to hear in their own language "about God's deeds of power" (v. 11).

The Pentecost story reversed the Tower of Babel story (Genesis 11:1–9). In that story an idolatrous use of one language led to babbling confusion. In the Pentecost story the Spirit worked through many languages to proclaim a message that led to new community and communication.

Peter's Pentecost sermon had to distinguish between drunken speech and speech that fulfilled the prophecy from Joel. That prophecy spoke of the outpouring of God's Spirit to cut through the barriers of gender and age (Acts 2:17–18) and equip people to prophesy, to "speak for" God. Such speaking was to lead to understanding, so that "everyone who calls on the name of God shall be saved" (v. 21). Those who would be saved would know a new relationship with God that would lead not to babbling confusion but to a new community of outreaching vision and dreams for God's world.

Respond to the Word

- What steps can the church take to be a more effective witness for God?
- What good news is the Spirit empowering you to proclaim this week? How will you respond to this power?

Go with the Word

Come! Holy Spirit, Come!

Come! Morning Star
Come! Cool of evening
Come! Dark night of the soul
Come! Source of illumination
Come! Essence of inspiration
Come! Swift as a sudden shower
Come! Sweet as a mountain spring
Come! Borne on chariots of cloud
Come! Riding the wings of the wind
Come! Breath of God
Come! Finger of God's right hand
Come! Song of the universe
Come! Dance of the distant stars
Come! Soul of all that lives
Come! Gift of all that gives
Come! Sign of healing and wholeness
Come! Silence within our prayer
Come! Everlasting Hope
Come! Tongues of fire and flame
Come! Love that never ends
Come! Life of the Living God
Come! Wisdom and Understanding
Come! Knowledge and Fortitude
Come! Caregiver, Comforter
Come! Laughter in the midst of tears
Come! Protector of the poor
Come! Friend of the utterly alone
Come! Known and yet Unknown
Come! Holy Spirit, come!
Come! Holy Spirit, come!

Miriam Therese Winter, *WomanPrayer, WomanSong* (New York: Crossroad, 1987). © Medical Mission Sisters. Used by permission of the Crossroad Publishing Company.

Hope Given

Hope does not disappoint us, because God's love has been poured into our hearts through the Holy Spirit that has been given to us.

Romans 5:5

Bible Reading: Romans 5:1–5

Additional Bible Readings: Proverbs 8:1–4, 22–31
                                      Psalm 8
                                      John 16:12–15

Enter the Word

- How might suffering affect one's faith?
- When have you experienced hope in the midst of suffering?

Read Romans 5:1–5, which prompts us to probe human suffering and to discover the Spirit's gift of hope. Consider the ways in which you or someone you know has experienced pain. Whether the pain was physical or emotional, temporary or lasting, reflect on how you or the person in pain coped.

Call to mind the places in your community or in the world where there is despair or suffering. You may find it helpful to look at a few headlines and pictures in a newspaper or news magazine to identify such places. Try to empathize with those who suffer. Imagine how faith and hope could bring a new perspective to their difficult situations.

Paul presents the readers of Romans with a simple formula: *Suffering produces endurance. Endurance produces character. Character produces hope. Hope does not disappoint.* However, as simple as it sounds or looks on paper, this chain of events requires strong faith. Reread Romans 5:1–5 and think about it in terms of your experiences with suffering. Imagine what you might say to Paul concerning his understanding that suffering ultimately leads to hope.

The reading from Romans celebrates the hope that we receive through the Holy Spirit. Read the additional scriptures for Trinity Sunday. Celebrate the hope the Holy Spirit has given you.

> *Empower me with your Spirit, O God, so that I might build endurance and character and hope. Amen.*

Engage the Word

- How could Paul, who demonstrated hope in the midst of his own sufferings, be a model for other Christians?

Paul wrote his letter to the Romans in the sixth decade of the first century, a few years before his death. One New Testament scholar, John Knox, has called it the most important single document in Christian history.

In this letter, Paul introduced himself to Christians in Rome. He wanted to overcome any misrepresentation of his views and establish a positive, supportive relationship with them. He sought to engage them and provide an understanding of the good news in Jesus Christ that could bridge differences and unite Jewish and Gentile Christians in Rome (note Romans 1:16–17).

Paul, a zealously religious Jew, had himself been a persecutor of Christians. For him, Jesus could not be the Messiah because a crucified Messiah was a contradiction. But then his encounter with Jesus, the risen Messiah, transformed his life. He came to see the death of Jesus as the deepest expression of God's love. In the cross God's love reached out fully to rebellious sinners to restore them to a new right relationship with God (see Romans 5:8).

In Romans 5:1, the word "therefore" points back to and rests on what precedes it, the death and resurrection of Jesus. He "was handed over to death for our trespasses and was raised for our justification" (Romans 4:25).

To justify, to "make right," is courtroom language. Here it means that God as judge has not passed a sentence of condemning judgment but of reconciling new life. God's outreaching love in

Jesus' death overcomes human wrongs, and God's power in Jesus' resurrection brings "newness of life" (note Romans 6:4).

To respond to this gift in Jesus Christ, to say "yes" to it, is what Paul means by "faith" (Romans 5:1). Faith is not believing a doctrine; it is entering a relationship. That new relationship Paul called peace, wholeness, and health with God (v. 1). It is not a human achievement but a matter of grace, God's gift, upon which life can stand (v. 2).

That standpoint is forward looking. In hope it looks forward to sharing the fullness of God's presence (v. 2) when all wrongs will be righted and suffering will be no more. But Paul knew full well in his own experience that suffering was still a part of human life. Faith does not save us from suffering. In fact, it may be, as with Paul, that devotion to Jesus Christ and his healing purpose produces suffering (v. 3).

But for Paul that suffering "produces endurance, and endurance produces character, and character produces hope" (vv. 3–4). This is not wishful thinking about the future. This hope does not disappoint because it is rooted in the love of God in Jesus.

The event of Jesus' cross and resurrection is past. It is the Holy Spirit that brings that past into the present and continues to pour God's love into human hearts. The New Testament has no doctrine of the Trinity, but Romans 5:1–5 combines powerfully the work of God in Christ through the Spirit. Later Trinitarian doctrine has its roots in the experience of Christians like Paul as presented in the New Testament.

Respond to the Word

- What can you, along with others, do this week to offer the hope of God's love to those who are suffering?
- What witness can you make about how hope has sustained you in times of suffering?

Go with the Word

How Shall I Pray?

How shall I pray?
Are tears prayers, Lord?
Are screams prayers,
     or groans
     or sighs
     or curses?
Can trembling hands be lifted up to you,
     or clenched fists
     or the cold sweat that trickles down my back
     or the cramps that knot my stomach?
Will you accept my prayers, Lord,
     my real prayers,
     rooted in the muck and mud and rock of my life and not
     just my pretty, cut-flower, gracefully arranged bouquet of
          words?
Will you accept me, Lord,
     as I really am,
     messed up mixture of glory and grime?

Only Speak the Word

The centurion sent friends to say to him, "Lord, do not trouble yourself, for I am not worthy to have you come under my roof; therefore I did not presume to come to you. But only speak the word, and let my servant be healed. When Jesus heard this he was amazed at him, and turning to the crowd that followed him, he said, "I tell you, not even in Israel have I found such faith."

Luke 7:6b–7, 9

Bible Reading: Luke 7:1–10

Additional Bible Readings: 1 Kings 8:22–23, 41–43
Psalm 96:1–9
Galatians 1:1–12

Enter the Word

- When have you been surprised by the faith of someone whom you thought was not religious?
- What example(s) can you think of when your own strong faith in God amazed others, perhaps even yourself?

As you read Luke 7:1–10, imagine that you are each of the characters in the story. See yourself as the slave in need of healing. Envision yourself as one of the Jewish elders who appeals to Jesus.

Put yourself in the place of the Roman centurion. Think about how you would have reacted, had you been Jesus, to the centurion's friends who told you not to come to the house. Consider how each character is affected by the faith of the centurion. Write in your spiritual journal about how this soldier's faith can be a model for your own. Pray that your faith might be increased.

Study 1 Kings 8:22–23, 41–43 and Psalm 96:1–9. Note how these passages include all persons in God's circle of care and concern. Also read Galatians 1:1–12 in which Paul warns the early church against falling from gospel faith into apostasy.

> *Increase my faith, Gracious God, that I might believe in your power to do all things. Amen.*

Engage the Word

- How might the story of the centurion have affirmed the faith of Luke's Gentile readers?

Most of the persons Jesus encountered in Luke's Gospel were among his own Jewish people. After all, Jesus was a Jew and he directed his mission first to his own people. That mission was to fulfill God's long love story with Israel.

Yet, Jesus did not come only for Jews. He was "good news of great joy for all the people" (Luke 2:10). He was, in the words of Simeon's song, "a light for revelation to the Gentiles and for glory to your people Israel" (Luke 2:32).

In today's reading from Luke 7:1–10, Jesus encounters a centurion, a Roman military officer. Though there was much hatred of the Roman occupying forces by the Jews, in this story it is Jewish elders who appeal to Jesus on behalf of the Roman officer and his highly valued, sick slave who is near death.

One of Luke's purposes in writing his Gospel and Acts toward the end of the first century was to create a climate in the Roman Empire that would not end in the persecution and destruction of Jesus' followers (as had happened in the year 70 C.E. with the destruction of Jerusalem by the Romans). For Luke, Christians were not anti-Empire; they were pro-Good News for everyone.

He wanted to paint a positive picture in terms of the relationships among Jews, Christians, and Romans that would foster "peace on earth." The Jewish elders tell Jesus how the Roman officer is worthy of his healing power, "for he loves our people, and it is he who built our synagogue for us" (vv. 4–5).

The Roman officer did not deem himself worthy to come to Jesus nor have Jesus enter his home. So when Jesus drew near, he simply asked Jesus to "speak the word, and let my servant be healed" (v. 7). He even compares the authority of his word as a soldier with Jesus' authoritative word (v. 8).

Luke points to Jesus' amazement at this officer's faith, this foreigner of another race. He affirms that he has not found such faith even among the religionists of his own people. The word of Jesus, combined with such faith, led to good health for the sick slave. God's authoritative word is at work to heal, but it is connected to the response of, even for Jesus, a most surprising person.

In Jesus' parable of the good Samaritan, again it is the person who was regarded by the religious establishment as a foreigner, a person of mixed race, a religious heretic, who fulfills the law of compassion and love. Another surprising person!

Luke has a powerful understanding of Jesus as one who speaks God's authoritative and healing word, but that word does not happen in a vacuum. It happens in the presence of surprising persons who in faith receive and believe it, who break through imposed traditional barriers, and who demonstrate that Jesus' word is "good news of great joy for all the people" (Luke 2:10).

Today's reading from 1 Kings 8 lifts up the foreigner who comes and prays so that all peoples of the earth may know God's name (vv. 41–43); and today's psalm says, "Declare God's glory among the nations, God's marvelous works among all the peoples" (96:3).

Respond to the Word

- What might happen in your own community if just one or two people exhibited the strong faith of the centurion?
- What healing might take place in your own life if you placed greater faith in God?

Go with the Word

O Christ, the Healer, We Have Come

*O Christ, the healer, we have come
to pray for health, to plead for friends.
How can we fail to be restored
when reached by love that never ends?*

*From every ailment flesh endures
our bodies clamor to be freed.
Yet in our hearts we would confess
that wholeness is our deepest need.*

*In conflicts that destroy our health
we recognize the world's disease;
Our common life declares our ills.
Is there no cure, O Christ, for these?*

*Grant that we all, made one in faith,
in your community may find.
The wholeness that, enriching us,
shall reach and prosper humankind.*

Young Man, Rise

He was his mother's only son, and she was a widow; and with her was a large crowd from the town. When the Lord saw her, he had compassion for her and said to her, "Do not weep." Then he came forward and touched the bier, and the bearers stood still. And he said, "Young man, I say to you, rise!"

Luke 7:12b–14

Bible Reading:	Luke 7:11–17
Additional Bible Readings:	1 Kings 17:8–24
	Psalm 146 or Psalm 30
	Galatians 1:11–24

Enter the Word

- When has God lifted you or a loved one from suffering?
- From what trial or illness do you need to be lifted now?

Suffering and physical death have been part of the human experience since the days of Adam and Eve. Thus, the death of the widow's son, as recorded in Luke 7, was certainly not an unusual event. However, in the midst of the widow's sorrow, the compassionate Jesus miraculously raised this man from the dead.

Jesus lifts us up to new life as well. Read Luke 7:11–17 and the words to the hymn "Out of the Depths I Call," found at the end of this lesson. Prayerfully state your own needs and wait patiently for God's gracious reply.

As you study the additional readings from 1 Kings 17:8–24, Psalm 146, Psalm 30, and Galatians 1:11–24, note how these passages highlight the idea of new life, either physically, as seen in Elijah's raising of the widow's son, or spiritually, as recorded in Paul's account of his new life in Christ.

> *In the midst of trials, illness, and death, lift me up, O God, to new life in you. Amen.*

Engage the Word

- How might Luke's understanding of Jesus' resurrection have helped readers see possibilities for newness in their lives?

Among the four Gospels, there are many stories of Jesus' healing in his ministry, but there are only two specific stories where Jesus raises the dead. One is where Jesus raises Lazarus in John 11; the other is today's Bible reading from Luke 7:11–17 where Jesus raises a widow's son. In addition, Matthew 11:5 and Luke 7:22 make general statements about the dead being raised.

All of the Gospels were written some forty to sixty or so years after Jesus' death and resurrection. Thus all of them view their stories of Jesus' ministry through the lens of his cross and resurrection. Jesus' own resurrection probably provided the lens for Luke and John to see Jesus' power over death at work in his ministry.

Whereas last Sunday's reading from Luke 7:1–10 centered on Jesus and a male Roman officer, today's focuses on Jesus and a weeping widow. Luke frequently juxtaposes male and female texts to provide some gender balance; and in this case he also juxtaposes texts that show persons marginalized by the dominant society: a Gentile and a widow. Today's reading from Psalm 146 also speaks of the God "who upholds the orphan and the widow" (v. 9).

Luke also has a very strong interest in connecting the Hebrew Scriptures to Jesus (note Luke 24:27). Today's reading from 1 Kings 17 presents a kind of parallel to today's reading from Luke. There the prophet Elijah raises a widow's son from death to new life (vv. 17–24). The God at work to give life through Elijah is now at work to give life through Jesus.

For Luke, Jesus' concern for this weeping mother shows his deep compassion (v. 13). He acts with his word to give life to her son: "Young man, I say to you, rise!" (v. 14). The word "rise" (*egertheti*) is the same word used in the story of Jesus' resurrection (Luke 24:5), "Why do you look for the living among the dead? He is not here, but has risen [*egerthe*]." The one who himself has been raised to new life has the power to raise others to new life.

This is no ordinary, run-of-the-mill event. As the once dead youth began to speak and Jesus gave him back to his mother, "Fear seized all of them [the large crowd]; and they glorified God, saying, 'A great prophet has risen [*egerthe*] among us!' and 'God has looked favorably on God's people!' " (v. 16).

What happens when such an amazing thing occurs? For Luke, with his deep concern for a message of good news that is to reach *all* people, "This word about Jesus spread throughout Judea and all the surrounding country" (v. 17).

The word of Jesus to the young man, "Rise," is not only a word to conquer death. It is a word of life in the midst of the "deathly" experiences we know now, which cry out for the compassion and life-giving presence of the risen Jesus. In today's reading from Psalm 30, the psalmist prays to God, "You brought up my soul from Sheol, restored me to life from among those gone down to the Pit" (v. 3). In Jesus, the life-restoring God is again at work with compassion and death-denying power, in Luke's time and in ours.

Respond to the Word

- In what ways can the community of faith offer new life to those who are suffering from "deathly" experiences, such as addiction, loneliness, or terminal illness?
- What compassionate action can you take this week to help someone experience the life-giving presence of Jesus?

Go with the Word

Out of the Depths I Call

Out of the depths I call,
to God I send my cry:
Oh, hear my supplicating voice
and graciously reply.

For you my soul still waits
with patience undeterred;
My hopes are on your promise built,
your neverfailing word.

My fainting spirit longs
for your enlivening ray,
More eager than the morning watch
to greet the dawning day.

Let Israel trust in God,
whose mercy boundless grows,
The plenteous source and spring
from whom redemption ever flows.

A New Version of the Psalms of David, ed. Nahum Tate and Nicholas
Brady, 1696; alt., in The New Century Hymnal (Cleveland, Ohio: The
Pilgrim Press, 1995), 483. Text Alterations copyright © 1995 by The
Pilgrim Press. Used by permission.

An Alabaster Jar

Then turning toward the woman, Jesus said to Simon, "Do you see this woman? I entered your house; you gave me no water for my feet, but she has bathed my feet with her tears and dried them with her hair. You gave me no kiss, but from the time I came in she has not stopped kissing my feet. You did not anoint my head with oil, but she has anointed my feet with ointment. Therefore, I tell you, her sins, which were many, have been forgiven; hence she has shown great love. But the one to whom little is forgiven, loves little." Then Jesus said to her, "Your sins are forgiven."

Luke 7:44–48

Bible Reading:	Luke 7:36–8:3
Additional Bible Readings:	1 Kings 2:1–10 (11–14), 15–21a 2 Samuel 11:26–12:10, 13–15 Psalm 5:1–8 or Psalm 32 Galatians 2:15–21

Enter the Word

- In what ways might people show their devotion to others?

- How do you respond to someone who has forgiven you?

Recall times when you longed to be forgiven. Remember how you expressed such a need. Reflect on how you knew you had been forgiven and your response to that forgiveness.

Perhaps you desire forgiveness now. Psalm 5:1–8 and Psalm 32 may help you focus on your need for forgiveness. Pray. Be patient in waiting for God. Experience a sense of forgiveness.

Read Luke 7:36–8:3. Try to relate your experiences of forgiveness to those of the woman.

Read the additional scriptures, which also demonstrate the larger theme of forgiveness and the awareness that one has been forgiven. First Kings 2:1–10 (11–14), 15–21a reports on the death of David and the consolidation of Solomon's power. Second Samuel 11:26–12:10, 13–15 tells of the judgment against David after he caused Uriah to be killed and of David's remorse for his sin. Galatians 2:15–21 repeats the theme of salvation by faith and the futility of attempting to save oneself by actions.

> *Let me pour myself out before you, O God, that I may*
> *be blessed with the forgiveness and peace of faith. Amen.*

Engage the Word

- What effect might this story have had on Luke's community, a group that stood outside the boundaries of Judaism?

The Gospel of Luke shows a deep concern for societal and religious outcasts. Luke wanted to proclaim the inclusiveness of God's reign. It meant outreach to outcast shepherds in the Christmas story and to a convicted criminal and crucifying soldiers at the cross. It meant outreach to cheating Rome-collaborating tax collectors and despised Samaritans. It meant outreach to women and children and to sinners who did not keep all the religious rules.

What precedes today's reading tells how Jesus got in trouble with religious leaders for eating with tax collectors and sinners (Luke 7:34). These latter received John the Baptist's baptism of repentance and forgiveness; the religious leaders rejected it (7:29–30).

Today's reading continues the contrast between a religious Pharisee and a sinful woman at a meal. Jesus accepted dinner invitations with religious leaders too (note also 14:1). He included them in his company, but he did not hesitate to challenge their exclusiveness (see Luke 14:7–14).

In Luke's moving story, the sinful woman came into the dinner party with her alabaster jar. (Alabaster is a finely granulated variety of white, translucent gypsum used for ornamental objects.) She bathed Jesus feet with her tears, dried them with her hair, kissed his feet, and anointed them with ointment.

The Pharisee Simon expected that Jesus as a prophet would know what kind of despicable sinner she was and reject her. But Jesus told Simon a story that forced him to answer for himself a question about the respective love of two debtors whose debts were canceled (vv. 40–43). His answer made him confront his callous response to the woman and her way of expressing love.

Jesus then went on to what must have been for Simon a painful comparison between himself and the woman (vv. 44–46). Though Jesus was speaking to Simon, he turned toward the woman. Jesus' focus was on her, even as he spoke to Simon. Her extravagant love was a response to Jesus' forgiveness ("letting go") of her many sins. She sensed forgiveness even before Jesus put it into words (v. 48).

Simon's friends at the table raised a question about the identity of this Jesus who forgave sins. After all, only God can forgive sins. But in recounting this question, Luke wanted to point to God and God's reign at work in Jesus. Jesus' authority to forgive sins is not his but God's. He spoke God's forgiveness.

Jesus called the woman's loving response "faith" (v. 50). Faith says "yes" to God's forgiveness. This response appropriated God's gift and saved her. It made her well and whole in her relationship with God, and she could "go in peace." She could go back to her daily life with a new sense of health and wholeness because her life had touched and been transformed by Jesus.

Respond to the Word

- How can you show compassion to someone who has wronged you?
- Who will you ask to forgive you this week?

Go with the Word

Anointing

We too have alabaster boxes
to be broken in the trust
that what we share will not be judged
in terms of vain conceit.
Rejoiced in rather
in the open way of One
who poured the precious oil
his own life to make
all other gifts complete.

J. Barrie Shepherd, "Anointing" (excerpt), in *alive now!*, March/April 1993, 12. Used by permission of the author.

One in Christ

As many of you as were baptized into Christ have clothed yourselves with Christ. There is no longer Jew or Greek, there is no longer slave or free, there is no longer male and female; for all of you are one in Christ Jesus. And if you belong to Christ, then you are offspring of Abraham and Sarah, heirs according to the promise.

Galatians 3:27–29

Bible Reading: Galatians 3:23–29

Additional Bible Readings: 1 Kings 19:1–4 (5–7), 8–15a
                                     or Isaiah 65:1–9
                                   Psalm 42 and 43 or Psalm 22:19–28
                                   Luke 8:26–39

Enter the Word

- What does the phrase "one in Christ" mean to you?
- Christ has broken down all barriers between people. How might that knowledge reshape your relationships with others?

As you read Galatians 3:23–29 notice the vivid pictures that Paul's words paint. Through baptism we "clothe" ourselves in Christ. Ponder what that means in your life. You may want to put on a garment to symbolically "clothe" yourself in Christ.

Look again at verses 28–29, which describe a new concept of

community, one of mutuality and unity, that Christ brings. Recall an incident you witnessed or experienced because of racial barriers or religious stereotypes. Replay the incident in your mind. Imagine that Jesus were present to remove those barriers. Visualize the incident as it might have happened if those who were involved had recognized that all are one in Christ.

As you read the additional scriptures, notice that God can break down any barriers. Luke tells the story of a man with demons whom Jesus delivered. The psalmist is certain that God is able to heal. God is also ready to care for us, even in seemingly impossible circumstances, as Elijah discovered.

> *Tear down the walls, O God, that separate me from you and keep me from seeing your image in others. Amen.*

Engage the Word

- Why might Paul have emphasized oneness in Christ to the early church?

In his letter to the Galatians, Paul had to defend both his apostleship and his understanding of the good news. The two were closely related because it was precisely his call to preach the gospel that made him an apostle.

But there were some Jewish Christians, the Judaizers, who wanted the gospel to be Jesus Christ plus the law of Moses (see Galatians 3:1–2). They challenged Paul's credentials because he did not receive his authority from the Jerusalem church, but from the risen Christ himself (see 1:11–12). Paul nevertheless wanted to be on good terms with the Jerusalem church and share the mission with them (2:9). He wanted unity among them in Christ.

For Paul, the law had its place (Galatians 3:19–22), but keeping the law could never be a means to a relationship with God. Keeping the law was a response to the liberating grace of the Exodus (note Exodus 20:2 which precedes the Ten Commandments). And for Paul, the gospel had its roots in the promise to Abraham that preceded the giving of the law (3:8–10, 17–18). But now, for him, the gospel that was declared beforehand to Abraham centered in Jesus Christ (3:22).

Paul used the phrase "before faith came" (Galatians 3:23). But in the next sentence he wrote, "until Christ came" (v. 24). For Paul, one cannot speak about faith without speaking about Christ. For him, the response of faith included that to which one responded, namely God's deed in Jesus.

Before Christ came, Paul believed that the law served as a disciplinarian (Galatians 3:24–25), the guardian who would take a child to school (note also 4:1–2). But with the coming of Christ, those who respond in faith are children of God (v. 26).

The public act that acknowledges this new faith relationship is baptism. There, the baptized are clothed with Christ. Now each baptized person can say with Paul, "It is no longer I who live, but it is Christ who lives in me" (Galatians 2:19–20). Christ becomes the identity of each Christian.

That means all prior identities are submerged in that new identity. "There is no longer Jew or Greek . . . slave or free . . . male and female; for all of you are one in Christ Jesus" (Galatians 3:28). In Christ the barriers are down in terms of ethnic background, social class, and gender. Life in Christ is to break all subordinating patterns and create a new mutuality and unity.

This belonging to Christ means also being offspring of Abraham and heirs of the promise to him. It was the promise to Abraham that not only Jews but "all the Gentiles [nations] shall be blessed in you" (Galatians 3:8; see Genesis 12:3; 18:18).

The coming of Jesus Christ was no isolated historical event. It became the climax of a long history that intends to break down all human barriers and tie all peoples together in a new community of God's grace. It is not a community to be achieved by human rule-keeping. It is a community to be received by faith in the Chosen Child of God, who loved and gave himself for all (Galatians 2:20).

Respond to the Word

- What barriers exist within a group you belong to? How can you help to break down these walls?
- What can you do this week to be more open to people who are different from you?

Go with the Word

Like the Murmur of the Dove's Song

To the members of Christ's body,
to the branches of the Vine,
to the church in faith assembled,
to its midst as gift and sign;
Come, Holy Spirit, come.

With the healing of division,
with the ceaseless voice of prayer,
with the power to love and witness,
with the peace beyond compare;
Come, Holy Spirit, come.

Freedom to Love and Serve

**For you were called to freedom, brothers and sisters;
only do not use your freedom as an opportunity for self-
indulgence, but through love serve one another. For the
whole law is summed up in a single commandment,
"You shall love your neighbor as yourself."**

Galatians 5:13–14

Bible Reading:	Galatians 5:1, 13–18
Additional Bible Readings:	1 Kings 2:1–2, 6–14
	or 1 Kings 19:15–16, 19–21
	Psalm 77:1–2, 11–20 or Psalm 16
	Luke 9:51–62

Enter the Word

- How do you define "freedom"?
- How does God's love prompt you to serve others?

Find a comfortable place and, with Bible in hand, close your
eyes and try to recall experiences such as the following: the last
time you took your shoes off to walk through a puddle or a creek; a
quiet afternoon with a special friend; a worship service that filled
your heart with song and carried you through the week; a time you
laughed so hard you cried; a gift (a bouquet of dandelions, a picture, a smile) given to you by a small child. Choose one of these or
another pleasant memory.

Read Galatians 5:1: "For freedom Christ has set us free." Joy comes with freedom—the freedom to splash in a puddle; the freedom to laugh out loud; the freedom to dwell with a friend in peace and harmony; the freedom to receive a gift of love.

After a few moments of rest in Paul's words, read all of today's scripture from Galatians 5:1, 13–18. Some of these words you may know by heart: "You shall love your neighbor as yourself." Remember a moment when you gave of yourself in love. This may be the same memory recalled a moment ago. Remember how you felt the last time you visited a friend in the hospital. You gave of yourself. Repeat those words of the heart, "you shall love your neighbor as yourself," as you dwell with the memory of love given through your service to others.

Also read today's additional scriptures—1 Kings 2:1–2, 6–14, 1 Kings 19:15–16, 19–21, Psalm 77:1–2, 11–20, Psalm 16, and Luke 9:51–62—and consider how they relate to today's lesson.

> *Help me, O God, to share your gift of love by serving others as Jesus did. Amen.*

Engage the Word

- What barriers might Paul's message have broken down in his day, and in ours as well?

The Bible reading for today (like last week's) comes from Paul's letter to the Galatians. You may want to look again at last week's "Engage the Word" section for a brief overview of the Galatians' situation that Paul addressed.

In chapters 1–4, Paul defended his apostleship and, to meet what he saw as a distortion of the gospel, presented his view of the gospel of Jesus' death and resurrection. He saw it as a barrier-breaking message (3:28), rooted in the inclusive promise to Abraham, now to be received by faith in Jesus Christ.

In chapters 5–6, Paul moved to more ethical implications and applications of that faith. Chapter 5 begins with the strong words, "For freedom Christ has set us free." Paul had to warn the Galatians not to fall back into the slavery of making the law (including circumcision) part of the gospel. He wrote that "the only thing that counts is faith working through love" (5:6).

Apparently some had accused him of preaching circumcision. But that charge made no sense if he was persecuted for not preaching it. To preach circumcision as a means of justifying one's relationship to God was to remove the offense, the scandal, of the cross. The relationship with God was not a matter of human action; it was a matter of God's grace and gift of love. Paul's anger at the charges against him came out strongly: "I wish those who unsettle you would castrate themselves" (v. 12).

This statement immediately precedes the continuing verses of today's reading. There Paul returned to his freedom theme. Freedom in Christ did not mean license to do whatever one pleased. It was not an "opportunity for self-indulgence" (v. 13).

Instead, it meant serving one another in love. It was the freedom to love. The whole law was fulfilled in the commandment "You shall love your neighbor as yourself" (Leviticus 19:18; note also Romans 13:8–10). There was to be no biting and devouring and consuming one another (Galatians 5:15).

Paul called for life by the Spirit, not by the flesh—that is, life directed toward and empowered by God, not directed toward and serving oneself (vv. 16–17). God's people are internally motivated by God's Spirit of love, not an externally imposed law (v. 18).

Those who belong to Jesus Christ (and his crucifixion; note 2:19–20) have crucified the old self-indulgent life. They live and are guided by the Spirit to show the love that builds and enriches human relationships (vv. 24–25).

God in love chose freely to send Jesus to redeem human beings and adopt them as children (Galatians 4:4–5). To respond to the freedom of such love is to live with a freedom to serve and "love your neighbor as yourself."

Respond to the Word

- What specific action can you take with others this week to serve those who need to feel God's gift of love?
- Look carefully at Jacob Lawrence's painting. How can the seated adult figure be a role model for you as you love and serve others this week?

Go with the Word

Jacob Lawrence, *Men Exist for the Sake of One Another. Teach Them
Then or Bear with Them*, 1958, National Museum of American Art,
Washington, D.C. (Art Resource, N.Y.). Used by permission.

As a Mother Comforts Her Child

As a mother comforts her child, so I will comfort you;

you shall be comforted in Jerusalem.

Isaiah 66:13

Bible Reading: Isaiah 66:10–14

Additional Bible Readings: 2 Kings 5:1–14
Psalm 30 or Psalm 66:1–9
Galatians 6:(1–6) 7–16
Luke 10:1–11, 16–20

Enter the Word

- What traits do you associate with a mother?
- Which of these motherly traits do you connect with God?

Although most of us have been taught to think of God as "father," this image reveals only part of the Bible's rich understanding of the nature of God. As you read Isaiah 66:10–14, be open to maternal images of God. Make a list of the images you find in this passage. If this idea of a maternal side of God is new to you, reflect on how these feminine images of God expand your understanding of who God is and how God relates to humanity.

Now think of a difficult situation in your own life at this moment. Reread Isaiah 66:10–14, hearing these words as if God is speaking directly to you. Allow the comforting voice you hear to be that of a woman.

Read today's additional scriptures. Second Kings 5:1–14 records how God, through the prophet Elisha, lovingly healed Naaman of a skin disease. Psalm 30 offers thanksgiving for healing, whereas

Psalm 66:1–9 offers thanks for the loving goodness that God has shown toward Israel. In the reading from Galatians 6:(1–6) 7–16, Paul reminds Christians that they are to work for the good of all people. Finally, in Luke 10:1–11, 16–20, Jesus demonstrates love by sending out witnesses to proclaim God's good news.

As you reflect on all of these readings, consider how God's comforting love is present in your own life right now.

> *Mother God, Father God, comfort me with your tender touch and compassionate love. Amen.*

Engage the Word

- How might the idea of God's loving, maternal care have comforted those who had experienced exile in Babylon?

The Bible is filled with masculine images and language pertaining to God. It appears as if God's words in Genesis had been forgotten—"Let us make humankind in our image, according to our likeness. . . . So God created humankind in God's image . . . male and female God created them" (Genesis 1:26–27). Both female and male are born out of the image of God.

This does not mean that God is male and female. Ultimately God is beyond gender. But in using categories of human experience to speak about God, there is a need to balance male and female images. The scripture from Isaiah lifts up the female. God speaks through the prophet to Israel, "As a mother comforts her child, so I will comfort you" (Isaiah 66:13).

Many persons in Israel had been through the difficult time of exile in the foreign land of Babylon. They had suffered much. But when they returned home to their land and the city of Jerusalem, the time of mourning was over. The time of rejoicing with Jerusalem had come (v. 10).

The verses that precede the reading from Isaiah employ female images to speak of Jerusalem: labor and birth, womb and deliverance (vv. 7–9). The reading continues such female images by speaking of the people as nursing at Jerusalem's consoling breasts and drinking from her glorious bosom (v. 11).

These female images for Jerusalem have their source in the God who says, "As a mother comforts her child, so I will comfort you;

you shall be comforted in Jerusalem" with her consoling breasts. The fourteenth-century female mystic Julian of Norwich could speak of being "suckled at the breasts of Christ."

One verse in Isaiah 66:10–14 combines the most grandiose with the most intimate. On the one hand, it speaks of Jerusalem's prosperity and overflowing wealth. And then, on the other, "you shall nurse and be carried on her arm, and dandled on her knees" (v. 12). Economic well-being is joined with motherly care.

Isaiah 66:10–14 begins on the note of rejoicing—an end to mourning. Psalm 30 also reflects this theme. "Weeping may linger for the night, but joy comes with the morning" (v. 5). "You have turned my mourning into dancing; you have taken off my sackcloth and clothed me with joy" (v. 11). Though "exile" was part of Israel's experience and is part of all human experience, God's desire for human life is joy, a joy rooted in the God who comforts us "as a mother comforts her child."

Another of the readings for today points to a young Hebrew girl held captive in Syria. If it had not been for her, the mighty Syrian warrior Naaman would never have known healing from his leprosy through the prophet Elisha (see 2 Kings 5:2–3).

It is important not only to recover female images for God but also to remember the many female servants of God in the Bible. God shows no partiality. Patterns of either male or female dominance have been broken. As Paul wrote, "There is no longer male and female; for all of you are one in Christ Jesus" (Galatians 3:28).

Respond to the Word

- How might your faith be broadened and enriched by thinking of God in both masculine and feminine terms?
- What difference would such an understanding make in your life this week?

Go with the Word

Like a Loving Mother

Loving God,
we are your children.
We know that you
have many children and
that you care for each one
like a loving mother.
Help us to be open to
your loving embrace.
We believe, dear God,
that you are greater
than any words we can use
to indicate your presence.
Sometimes we define
you in narrow terms.
Help us to find
fresh ways to think of you.
You are mother;
you are father;
you are grandmother;
you are grandfather.
And, great God,
you are even more.

From *The Inviting Word Older Youth Learner's Guide,* Year One
(Cleveland, Ohio: United Church Press, 1994), 98. © 1994 by United
Church Press. Used by permission.

Hard Words

Then Amos answered Amaziah, "I am no prophet, nor a prophet's son; but I am a herdsman, and a dresser of sycamore trees, and God took me from following the flock, and God said to me, 'Go, prophesy to my people Israel.' "

Amos 7:14–15

Bible Reading:	Amos 7:7–17
Additional Bible Readings:	Deuteronomy 30:9–14
	Psalm 82 or Psalm 25:1–10
	Colossians 1:1–14
	Luke 10:25–37

Enter the Word

- What "hard words" are the prophets of our day proclaiming?
- How do prophetic words guide your own faith journey?

Read Psalm 82. Think of times in your life when you have felt that justice was denied. Perhaps you cried out for justice by organizing a group to deal with an issue. The writer of Psalm 82 expressed his cry through prayer.

Read the parable of the Good Samaritan in Luke 10:25–37. As you read, think of your neighbors and others in need of your care. Ponder your response to the question, "And who is my neighbor?"

Now read Amos 7:7–17. Amos has a very different style of

communicating than the psalmist or the writer of the gospel, but the basic thirst for justice is the same. His words convey a strong sense of right and wrong and a need for God's intervention to bring justice to the world. Remember the cry for justice in Psalm 82 as you read Amos' words.

The prophet urged God's people to repent. Although Amos called individuals to change, he was also concerned with the need for society as a whole to change. Think of places in our society that are in need of change. Imagine the consequences of failure to change. Envision the benefits of such change.

Now read Psalm 25:1–10 and Colossians 1:1–14 and make connections with the passages you have already explored.

> *Open my ears to the prophetic words that call me to repentance so that I might change my ways, O God. Amen.*

Engage the Word

- How do the words of the prophet confront God's people and call them to repentance as individuals and as a body?

The Bible holds together two important parts of human life, the personal and the social. The one can portray God as intimately as a mother comforting her child (as in last Sunday's reading). The other can depict God with a plumb line (a tool to show what is straight) to judge the crookedness of a nation as in today's reading from Amos (note also Psalm 82:1–4). God cares not only about individuals' personal relationship with God and others but also about a nation's social policies. God speaks through Amos, "let justice roll down like waters, and righteousness like an everflowing stream" (Amos 5:24).

In the eighth century before Jesus' coming, God called Amos from his herds in the Southern Kingdom of Judah to prophesy ("speak for" God) in the Northern Kingdom of Israel. His hearers might well have been glad as he thundered against the wrongs of Israel's neighboring nations (chapters 1–2), but then he spoke against the wrongs of Israel itself (beginning in chapter 3).

How could God judge Israel, God's own chosen people, for its social and economic injustice? Because God had led them out of social and economic injustice in Egypt. With that beginning, it is difficult to imagine that they could perpetrate any injustice against others. But they did, and God would punish them (see Amos 3:1–2).

Israel was in fact overrun by Assyria in 722 B.C.E., and many of its people were carried into exile. Amos' prophecy of doom against Israel did happen (note Amos 7:9, 11, 17). As God's prophet he announced that God's hand of judgment would fall upon those who failed to stand for righteousness and justice.

Surprisingly, the one who resisted Amos' message was Amaziah, a religious leader and priest. He complained to King Jeroboam about Amos (vv. 10–11). Not only that, Amaziah told Amos to go home and prophesy there but never again in Amaziah's domain at the Temple and king's sanctuary at Bethel (vv. 12–13; Bethel means "house of God"; note the words about Bethel in Amos 5:5–7).

Thus it was a religious leader who tried to thwart Amos' prophetic message. The one who in God's name ought to stand for righteousness and justice was the very one who sought to silence God's prophet. The nonprofessional prophet had to speak against the professional priest. God's people needed to hear a call to repentance for their injustice. Similarly, in today's reading from Luke, the priest and Levite passed by. It was the despised Samaritan who showed mercy. If religious leaders will not speak against injustice, God will call courageous laity to do so.

Amos declared that God abhors religion that is defended or practiced without justice: "I hate, I despise your festivals, and I take no delight in your solemn assemblies. . . . Take away from me the noise of your songs. . . . But let justice roll down like waters, and righteousness like an everflowing stream" (Amos 5:21–24). These hard words continue to challenge us today.

Respond to the Word

- What injustices do you and others in your community need to address? How will you work together to do that?
- If you were sent to prophesy on behalf of God, where would you go and what would you say this week?

Go with the Word

Have Mercy on Us

Because we have seen pain without being moved,
because we forget your love with solemn pride,
because we pass by happy before poverty and sadness,
Lord have mercy,
Lord have mercy,
have mercy on us.

For speaking of love without loving our sister or brother,
for speaking of faith without living your word,
because we live without seeing our personal evil, our sin,
Christ have mercy,
Christ have mercy,
have mercy on us.

For our tranquility in our affluent life,
for our great falseness in preaching about poverty,
for wanting to make excuses for injustice and misery,
Lord have mercy,
Lord have mercy,
have mercy on us.
Amen.

United Church of Christ Book of Worship (New York: United Church of Christ Office for Church Life and Leadership, 1986), 532–33. Used by permission.

Justice for the Poor

Then God said to me, "Hear this, you that trample on the needy, and bring to ruin the poor of the land, buying the poor for silver and the needy for a pair of sandals, and selling the sweepings of the wheat." God has sworn by the pride of Jacob: Surely I will never forget any of their deeds.

Amos 8:4, 6–7

Bible Reading:	Amos 8:1–12
Additional Bible Readings:	Genesis 18:1–10a
	Psalm 52 or Psalm 15
	Colossians 1:15–18
	Luke 10:38–42

Enter the Word

- What are some modern examples of justice and injustice?
- What is your personal attitude toward those who are poor?

The Bible challenges us to examine our attitudes and treatment of those who are poor. Read Amos 8:1–12, which prompts us to hear God's call for justice for the poor and to examine our response to that call. As you read, imagine that you are present, listening to Amos' words. Reflect on how these words confront your own attitudes and practices. You may wish to write a response to Amos in a spiritual journal.

Broaden your individual response by considering how the church might react to Amos' indictment. Think too about how Amos' words challenge society to treat the poor with justice. Brainstorm ideas for changing unjust social and economic systems.

Continue your study by reading the additional scriptures. Genesis shows the importance of hospitality, for we may be unaware of God's presence in our midst. Psalm 52 promises "just desserts" for the wicked. Psalm 15 points out that those who are admitted into the worshiping community must have high moral standards, including a sense of justice. Luke 10:38–42, the familiar story of the sisters Mary and Martha, reminds us that human understanding of fairness and justice may be quite different from God's.

> *Just and loving God, empower me to help bring about the personal, social, and economic justice that you intend for all people. Amen.*

Engage the Word

- What effect might Amos' words have had on those who were poor? How might the same words have affected those who exploited the poor?

Often in the Hebrew Scriptures the prophets spoke with images. In last week's reading, Amos spoke of the plumb line. In today's he speaks of a basket of summer fruit. For Amos, both were symbols of God's judgment upon an unjust Israel. The basket of summer fruit points to the harvest season, at which time God as harvester judges the fruit. The time is ripe, for "the end has come" (v. 2).

Both readings from Amos have to do with social justice. The plumb line, with its measure of what is straight, exposes a nation's crookedness. The basket of summer fruit points to a nation's deeds, unworthy and ripe for judgment.

Last week's reading from Amos does not get specific. In contrast, today's passage speaks in very concrete terms about those who trample on people in need and ruin those who are poor (v. 4). It speaks of those who want to be finished with religious festivals and

Sabbaths so they can get back to business and exploit people through corrupt practices (v. 5). It even speaks of buying persons who are needy and poor (v. 6; note also Psalm 15:5).

But God swears an oath by what Israel is supposed to stand for ("the pride of Jacob"—freedom and faithfulness) that God will not forget these deeds (v. 7). Such deeds make the land tremble and everyone mourn. They make for flooding upheaval like the rising and tossing and sinking of the Nile River (v. 8).

Where do such deeds of exploitation lead? God spoke through Amos about the sun going down at noon and bringing darkness to the earth during the day (v. 9). Such exploitation affects even nature itself. Though one cannot speak of smog in the time of Amos, the biblical image makes one think of the cloud hanging over many of the world's cities today. To exploit people and nature leads to a time when day is no more.

And it all leads to much mourning: "The songs of the temple shall become wailings" and "dead bodies shall be many, cast out in every place" (v. 3). Feasts shall turn into mourning and songs into lamentations with people in sackcloth and with shaved heads, a bitter mourning as for an only child (v. 10). The final verses of the reading from Amos speak of famine—not a famine of bread or a thirst for water, but a famine of hearing the words of God (v. 11). People wander everywhere seeking these words, but they do not find them (v. 12).

Amos lived more than seven hundred years before Christ's coming. Yet his words still apply to many places in our world today. The poor are still being treated unjustly and exploitation still leads to death and mourning.

Respond to the Word

- What situations in your community, country, and the world need to be confronted by Amos' prophetic words?
- How will you respond to at least one of these situations in the coming week?

Go with the Word

Jesus Is Crucified

Many of us are crucified with you—abandoned in jails, on trash heaps, in the streets, in cardboard shelters, under bridges, with nothing to eat but what others throw away. May we say with you, "Father, forgive them, for they do not know what they do."

At the same time, there are those among us who crucify you still. We weep at the thought of the cruel persons who crucified you; but we continue to do the same thing, when we abandon our children, or the elderly, when we enjoy our coffee with sugar while farm workers are being subjected to a cruel, unjust exploitation, when we make fun of the imaginary inferiority of blacks, the poor, or other races. Forgive us, Lord, for all the times we have lynched, scourged, tortured, and murdered the poor, blacks, or immigrants, when we have robbed them of their lands, despised them for their customs, and expelled them from our countries because we want no "foreigners" among us.

Lord, stir up in me a great sorrow and sense of scandal at having crucified you by abusing the weak in our country, and grant me a desire to change my life. Help me see the invisible wickedness of my people, that I may repent and begin to walk a new way. Lord, do not permit us to pursue the paths that crucify whole populations. Help us crucify our false values, that we may rise to new values. Lord, I know not the way. But you can do all things. You can accomplish this in me and in my people. Amen.

José Oscar Beozzo, in *Way of the Cross: The Passion of Christ in the Americas*, ed. Virgil Elizondo, trans. John Drury (Maryknoll: Orbis Books, 1992), 77–78.

The Prayer of Jesus

Jesus was praying in a certain place, and after he had finished, one of the disciples said to him, "Jesus, teach us to pray, as John taught his disciples." Jesus said to them, "When you pray, say: Father [and Mother], hallowed be your name. Your dominion come. Give us each day our daily bread. And forgive us our sins, for we ourselves forgive everyone indebted to us. And do not bring us to the time of trial."

Luke 11:1–4

Bible Reading: Luke 11:1–13

Additional Bible Readings: Hosea 1:2–10 or Genesis 18:20–32
Psalm 85 or Psalm 138
Colossians 2:6–15 (16–19)

Enter the Word

- What role does prayer play in your life?
- How does the Prayer of Jesus shape and support your own relationship with God?

Close your eyes and imagine a group gathered for worship. Listen to the sound of their voices saying the Prayer of Jesus. After a few moments of imagined listening, say the prayer by yourself, perhaps aloud. Be aware of how each phrase in the prayer touches you.

Read Luke 11:1 and envision yourself with Jesus. Read 11:2–13, noticing that the words likely differ from the version of the Prayer of Jesus you use. Reflect on how these differences may enrich the meaning of the prayer for you.

Now write the Prayer of Jesus from memory, leaving a blank line after each phrase. Then, on the blank lines, rewrite the prayer in your own words. Finally, read the prayer as it appears in the Aramaic Lord's Prayer, found on page 221.

Continue your study by reading two prayers from Psalms 85 and 138. In Genesis 18:20–32, Abraham intercedes for Sodom and Gomorrah. Colossians 2:6–15 (16–19) is a warning against false teachers. Hosea 1:2–10 describes the prophet's marriage to the unfaithful Gomer and the birth of their children.

> Holy be your name, O God, for you are the one to whom I lift my prayers in worship and praise. Amen.

Engage the Word

• How does Jesus' prayer serve as a model for the church?

Four of the readings for today involve prayer. Psalm 85:1–7 and Psalm 138 both are prayers. In the Genesis reading, Abraham prays. The scripture from Luke centers on prayer and includes Luke's version of the Prayer of Jesus (see Matthew 6:9–13 for the version used more commonly in church liturgies).

All the Gospels present Jesus as one who prayed, but Luke has the strongest emphasis on prayer. In comparing Luke with Mark and Matthew, Luke showed Jesus praying in a series of parallel texts, whereas Mark and Matthew do not (see for example, Luke 3:21; 5:16; 6:12; 9:18, 29).

As one who prayed, Jesus was a model for his first disciples. Luke wanted his community to see Jesus as a model for them too. They too were to be a community of prayer. In today's reading, Luke presented Jesus as praying (v. 1). His disciples asked him to teach them to pray as John the Baptist had taught his disciples (v. 1).

Luke's version of the Prayer of Jesus first adores God and then follows with four petitions. The word translated "hallowed" might be translated "holied" or "wholed." It honors God as holy and whole. Also, in the Bible, one's "name" expresses one's very nature. God's nature is to be whole and to make life whole. The prayer adores God before asking God for anything.

To ask for God's reign or kingdom is to ask God to transform life as Jesus had done. God's reign means healing and making persons, as well as nature, whole. It means good news to persons in poverty. It means reaching out to include those whom society has excluded. Such a reign was at work in Jesus (see Luke 4:18, 11:20, 17:20–21).

The three petitions that follow point to essential parts of human life. To pray for bread is to ask God to meet human hunger, not in a one-time handout, but "daily."

To pray for forgiveness involves personal relationships with both God and others. It asks God to "let go" of sins, of that which breaks relationships. But God's forgiveness is joined with human willingness to forgive others their indebtedness. Given Luke's concern for the poor, forgiving "indebtedness" may include overtones of "letting go" monetary debt.

The last petition was earlier translated "lead us not into temptation." It now reads "do not bring us to the time of trial" (with some ancient manuscripts adding "but rescue us from the evil one or evil"). The word translated "trial" or "temptation" links this petition to Jesus' temptation (Luke 4:2). Human life does involve struggle against evil. The sense of this petition is "do not bring us to any trial, testing, or temptation with which, by your empowering Spirit, we cannot cope." The apostle Paul wrote, "God is faithful, and God will not let you be tested beyond your strength" (1 Corinthians 10:13; note also James 1:13).

Today's Gospel reading calls for followers to be persistent in prayer (vv. 5–8) and tells God's response to such persistence—to asking, searching, knocking. God brings the gift of God's own Spirit to those who refuse to give up their petitions.

Respond to the Word

- With whom can you share the Prayer of Jesus this week?
- What commitment will you make to pray this prayer regularly?

Go with the Word

ܐܒܘܢ ܕܒܫܡܝܐ ܢܬܩܕܫ ܫܡܟ. ✴ ܬܐܬܐ ܡܠܟܘܬܟ. ܢܗܘܐ
ܨܒܝܢܟ: ܐܝܟܢܐ ܕܒܫܡܝܐ: ܐܦ ܒܐܪܥܐ. ✴ ܗܒ ܠܢ ܠܚܡܐ ܕܣܘܢܩܢܢ
ܝܘܡܢܐ. ✴ ܘܫܒܘܩ ܠܢ ܚܘܒܝܢ: ܐܝܟܢܐ ܕܐܦ ܚܢܢ ܫܒܩܢ ܠܚܝܒܝܢ. ✴ ܘܠܐ
ܬܥܠܢ ܠܢܣܝܘܢܐ: ܐܠܐ ܦܨܢ ܡܢ ܒܝܫܐ. ܡܛܠ ܕܕܝܠܟ ܗܝ ܡܠܟܘܬܐ
ܘܚܝܠܐ ܘܬܫܒܘܚܬܐ ܠܥܠܡ ܥܠܡܝܢ ܐܡܝܢ.

The Prayer of Jesus (Aramaic)

Abwoon d'bwashmaya
Nethqadash shmakh
Teytey malkuthakh
Nehwey tzevyanach aykanna d'bwashmaya aph b'arha.
Hawvlan lachma d'sunqanan yaomana.
Washboqlan khaubayn (wakhtahayn)
aykana daph khnan shbwoqan l'khayyabayn.
Wela tahlan l'nesyuna
Ela patzan min bisha.
Metol dilakhie malkutha wahayla wateshbukhta
l'ahlam almin.
Ameyn.

In God's Arms

Yet it was I who taught Ephraim to walk, I took them up in my arms; but they did not know that I healed them. I led them with cords of human kindness, with bands of love. I was to them like those who lift infants to their cheeks. I bent down to them and fed them.

Hosea 11:3–4

Bible Reading:	Hosea 11:1–11
Additional Bible Readings:	Ecclesiastes 1:2, 12–14; 2:18–23
	Psalm 107:1–9, 43
	or Psalm 49:1–12
	Colossians 3:1–11
	Luke 12:13–21

Enter the Word

- What feelings emerge when you realize that you are snuggled in God's arms?
- How have you perceived God's forgiving love in the midst of judgment?

Read Hosea 11:1–11, a passage that underscores both the judgment of God and God's tender care. As you read, see if any aspects of the relationship between God and Israel remind you of the parent/child relationship. Consider how these two relationships are both similar to and different from one another.

Recall an incident from your childhood that caused a parent pain. Remember how you felt when you realized how your behavior had affected your parent. Consider ways that you might be causing God pain like that of the pain a child might cause parents. If you are a parent, also remember a time when you felt pain on behalf of your child, just as God feels pain on our behalf. If you keep a spiritual journal, dialogue with God about the impact your attitudes and actions have on others and on God as well. Pray that God will give you the strength and wisdom to make necessary changes.

Also study the additional Bible readings. In Psalm 107 a group of pilgrims to Jerusalem give thanks for God's goodness and love that endures forever. Psalm 49 is a wisdom psalm that reminds the reader that life and wealth are both transient. Luke 12:13–21 includes the parable of the rich fool which, like Psalm 49, underscores the fleeting nature of life and wealth. In Colossians 3:1–11 Paul speaks of how those who are in Christ are to live.

> *Hold me, O God, in your loving arms that I may feel your tender compassion. Amen.*

Engage the Word

- How might the people of Hosea's day, who were suffering as a result of war with Assyria, have heard the prophet's words about God's coming judgment and promise of future restoration?

Hosea's words come from the eighth century B.C.E. prior to Assyria's overrunning the Northern Kingdom of Israel. He depicted God's agonizing over Israel's adulterous disloyalty and worship of other gods. The prophet moved from God's love to God's judgment and back again, from threats of destruction to promises of restoration. Hosea expresses God's feelings in some of the most passionate and moving writings in the entire Bible.

One sees both love and judgment in today's reading from Hosea 11. It begins with a beautiful portrayal of God's love and care (vv. 1–4), but then shifts to declaring God's judgment (vv. 5–7). Yet God cannot bear such judgment upon God's people, and it shifts back again to God's compassion (vv. 8–9) and finally to Israel's return home (vv. 10–11).

Through Hosea, God spoke of Israel as a child whom God called out of slavery in Egypt centuries earlier (v. 1). But the more God called them the more they turned from God to other gods (v. 2). God taught Ephraim as a child—taught the people of Israel to walk, took them up in God's arms, healed them, led them with kindness and love like those lifting infants to their cheeks, and fed them (vv. 3–4). Do any verses in the Bible present a more tender portrayal of God?

But then the voice of judgment falls. Because of their disloyalty to God, those whom God had led out of Egyptian bondage shall return there, as well as be ruled by Assyria (v. 5). Their cities shall be destroyed and their prattling priests consumed (v. 6). Because they have turned away, God would not restore them when they called (v. 7).

God just cannot stop there. God just cannot hand Israel over and make them like two destroyed cities. No, God's compassion grows warm and tender (v. 8). God will not, in anger, destroy them. After all, God is God and not a human being. God is the Holy One, the Healing One, who does not come to the city in wrath to destroy (v. 9; the original Hebrew here is uncertain).

As God roars like a lion, God's children finally follow after God, not other gods, and come home from Egypt and Assyria like birds and doves. God will bring them home (vv. 10–11).

Hosea would not agree with the writer of the reading for Proper 13 from Ecclesiastes that "All is vanity." He would agree much more with the psalmist that God's "steadfast love endures forever" (Psalm 107:1), though the psalm does not bypass life's struggles (see vv. 4–6). For writers like Hosea, God's love is not a sloppy love. God judges human idolatry, but God's last word is not wrath but "steadfast love."

Respond to the Word

- How can you and your community of faith bear witness to God's compassionate love, especially to those whose behaviors have caused pain for themselves, others, and God?
- In what ways does this reading renew or alter your own understanding of God's love and judgment?

Go with the Word

In God's Arms

To the property of motherhood belong nature, love, wisdom and knowledge, and this is God. For though it may be so that our bodily bringing to birth is only little, humble and simple in comparison with our spiritual bringing to birth, still it is [God] who does it in the creatures by whom it is done. The kind, loving mother who knows and sees the need of her child guards it very tenderly, as the nature and condition of motherhood will have. And always as the child grows in age and in stature, she acts differently, but she does not change her love. And when it is even older, she allows it to be chastised to destroy its faults, so as to make the child receive virtues and grace. This work, with everything which is lovely and good, our Lord performs in those by whom it is done. So [God] is our Mother in nature by the operation of grace in the lower part, for love of the higher part. And God wants us to know it, for [God] wants to have all our love attached to [God].

Julian of Norwich, *Showings*, trans. Edmund Colledge and James Walsh
(New York: Paulist Press, 1978), 299.

By Faith

Now faith is the assurance of things hoped for, the conviction of things not seen.

Hebrews 11:1

Bible Reading:	Hebrews 11:1–3, 8–16
Additional Bible Readings:	Isaiah 1:1, 10–20
	or Genesis 15:1–6
	Psalm 50:1–8, 22–23
	or Psalm 33:12–22
	Luke 12:32–40

Enter the Word

- How do you define the word "faith"?
- What role does faith play in your own life?

Begin by reading Genesis 15:1–6, the introduction to the story of Abram (renamed Abraham) and Sarai (later Sarah), people of faith. God instructed Abram to look to the stars as a way to imagine the number of descendants who would follow him. The gift God promised to Abram was astounding, and it took great faith to believe in that gift.

Now read Hebrews 11:1–3, 8–16. You may have heard these words before and perhaps know them by heart. If you have time, continue reading to the end of chapter 11. Reflect on the fact that you stand in a long line of people who acted on faith.

When you have finished reading, complete the following sentence: "By faith, [insert your name here] undertook the task of [insert your words here], so that [insert your words here]."

226

If you keep a journal, let these words be the starting point for a journal entry. If you prefer, take time to meditate and think about the relationship between your faith and a task that you have identified. You might also consider reading and reflecting on your denomination's statement of faith. Consider ways that your own faith and your work relate to the promises in the statement of faith.

Now explore how the additional readings from Isaiah 1:1 and 10–20, Psalm 50:1–8 and 22–23, Psalm 33:12–22, and Luke 12:32–40 might build up your own faith.

> *Increase my faith, O God, that I might respond to your call on my life. Amen.*

Engage the Word

*   What does "faith" mean to the writer of Hebrews?

The word "faith" is one of the major words in the Bible. Biblical writers use it with different meanings, however. For some, faith is the dynamic response to and trusting relationship with God. For others, faith is a system of doctrines to be confessed, as in creeds. For still others, faith is believing something we cannot prove but about which we have strong convictions. The last meaning is close to the way the letter to the Hebrews defines faith in today's Bible reading.

"Now faith is the assurance of things hoped for, the conviction of things not seen" (Hebrews 11:1, NRSV). "Faith gives substance to our hopes, and makes us certain of realities we do not see" (NEB). "Now faith is the substance of things hoped for, the evidence of things not seen" (KJV). These different translations all make clear that Hebrews' understanding of faith is oriented toward the future. It is confidence (from two Latin words meaning "with faith") in God's future.

In chapter 11, the writer of Hebrews looked back to a whole company of persons of faith from Hebrew Scriptures. Their faith was not some wishful thinking about the future. It was a confidence in God's future upon which they acted in the present. Such faith was not based on the human capacity to have faith. Rather it was based on God whose promises are faithful.

By such faith these ancestors received God's approval (v. 2).

The writer begins by setting a context for the faith of those persons by asking the church to have faith in God who created the world—all that is visible and invisible (v. 3).

Today's Bible reading skips over some spiritual ancestors of faith (vv. 4–7) and centers on the faith of Abraham. Today's additional Bible reading from Genesis is one that underlies Hebrews' depiction of Abraham as a person of faith. Abraham's sojourn was an act of faith in God. Abraham and Sarah set out uncertain about the promised land they would inherit (vv. 8–9).

Strikingly, the writer of Hebrews reinterpreted this earthly promised land as only temporary and foreign. The original Hebrew understanding was that the promise to inherit land was fulfilled in their occupation of Canaan. But the writer of Hebrews pointed to the inheritance as the future heavenly "city that has foundations, whose architect and builder is God" (v. 10).

Hebrews 11 points to another aspect of Abraham's faith: the faith that he and Sarah would have a child in their old age. This would lead to countless descendants (vv. 11–12). What is so important here is that through such descendants all the families of the earth were to be blessed (Genesis 12:3).

As the writer of Hebrews looked back on such people of faith, he wrote, "All of these died in faith without having received the promises." The writer understood God's final promise to be a heavenly home (vv. 13–14).

Israel's history provided many examples of persons who in faith responded to God's promises. They courageously endured all kinds of hardships by faith in God's future for life both in this world and beyond it.

Respond to the Word

- In what ways can you be a role model of faith for others?
- What is God calling you to do right now? How will faith empower your response?

Go with the Word

By Faith

Abraham's Farewell to Ishmael, sculpted by George Segal, suggests both uncertainty and faith. At left, Abraham embraces the son who was to be the future; Hagar (in foreground) faces the unknown of desert exile while Sarah (right background), mother-to-be of yet a different future, watches in silence. The artist depicts Abraham, Hagar, Ishmael, and Sarah facing uncertainty with conviction.

George Segal, *Abraham's Farewell to Ishmael,* 1987, painted plaster, 102" x 78" x 78", Sidney Janis Gallery, New York. © 1997 by George Segal/Licensed by VAGA, New York, N.Y. Photo courtesy Sidney Janis Gallery. Used by permission.

The Cloud of Witnesses

Therefore, since we are surrounded by so great a cloud of witnesses, let us also lay aside every weight and the sin that clings so closely, and let us run with perseverance the race that is set before us, looking to Jesus the pioneer and perfecter of our faith, who for the sake of the joy that was set before him endured the cross, disregarding its shame, and is seated at the right hand of the throne of God.

Hebrews 12:1–2

Bible Reading:	Hebrews 11:29–12:2
Additional Bible Readings:	Isaiah 5:1–7 　or Jeremiah 23:23–29 Psalm 80:1–2, 8–19 or Psalm 82 Luke 12:49–56

Enter the Word

- Who are some of the people that you envision in the cloud of witnesses?
- How does the remembrance of spiritual ancestors empower you to be more faithful?

Close your eyes and remember times you have entered a church sanctuary and felt the presence of family members who have worshiped there and filled the air with their faithfulness. Let your imagination draw you and those you recall into a circle. Imagine being in a sanctuary as you read Hebrews 12:1–2.

Next, imagine that biblical figures join your circle. Picture them quietly walking forward to join hands with your grandmother, the person who first welcomed you into your congregation, a favorite church school teacher, the church custodian, the youth who eagerly waits to receive communion

Read Hebrews 11:29–12:2. Imagine that you are reading it to this faithful "cloud of witnesses." Be aware of your feelings as you envision this company of the faithful alongside you.

Also study the additional readings from Isaiah 5:1–7, Jeremiah 23:23–29, Psalm 80:1–2, 8–19, Psalm 82, and Luke 12:49–56.

Thank you, God, for those who have guided me in my own faith journey. Let me be a witness to others. Amen.

Engage the Word

- What impact might the knowledge that they were surrounded by a "cloud of witnesses" have had on the early Christians?

In the Bible, faith is never a matter simply for an isolated individual. It involves a community of persons that stretches back into the past, embraces people in the present, and anticipates a fellowship in the future. Faith involves a "cloud of witnesses" to God's continuing faithfulness.

Today's Bible reading begins in the same chapter of the letter to the Hebrews as the reading for last week. The verses between them (Hebrews 11:17–28) continue to speak of Abraham and also spotlight other persons of faith—Isaac, Jacob, Joseph, and Moses. Today's reading also relates faith to the Exodus and Jericho events, as well as to Rahab, Gideon, Barak, Samson, Jephthah, David, and Samuel (vv. 29–32).

The passage then goes on to state some tremendous things that people of faith have accomplished (vv. 33–34) and the terrible things they have endured (vv. 35–38). Though tortured for their faith, their willingness to endure would lead to their obtaining a "better resurrection" (v. 35).

As the writer of Hebrews interpreted it, all these people, though commended for their faith, did not receive what God had promised (v. 39). What was promised was still in their future.

The writer believed that these persons who lived before Christ's coming would only be "made perfect" after Christ's coming. They would join the Christian writer of Hebrews and his readers (v. 40) in the goal of the promised heavenly city in the future (see Hebrews 11:10, 13–16 in last week's reading).

This union creates a solidarity between those living before and those living after Christ's coming. These persons of faith from the past are a great "cloud of witnesses" that surround people in the present (Hebrews 12:1). They too will share in that "better resurrection" (11:35) of Jesus Christ whom God "brought back from the dead" (13:20). Christians were not the first to have faith in God's promises. There is a prior great "cloud of witnesses" attested to in the Hebrew Scriptures.

So what are people in the present to do? They are to be faithful runners just as their spiritual predecessors were. The writer said to his readers, "Let us also lay aside every weight and the sin that clings so closely, and let us run with perseverance the race that is set before us" (Hebrews 12:1). A runner cannot run well with excess baggage and the energy-destroying sin of broken relationships with God and others.

And to whom are they to look in the race? The writer said "to Jesus the pioneer and perfecter of our faith" (v. 2). One translation has it, "our eyes fixed on Jesus, on whom faith depends from start to finish" (NEB). He could endure the shame of the cross to know the joy of sharing in God's power (v. 2).

The readers of the letter to the Hebrews confronted the temptation to deny their faith in the face of persecution (note Hebrews 12:3–4). Looking to Jesus and being supported by "so great a cloud of witnesses," they could have courage to be faithful in living in the present and to looking to God's future.

Respond to the Word

- In what new arenas can your congregation be witnesses for God in the community a large?
- How can you be a positive witness to someone this week?

Go with the Word

Not Alone

Here I stand, O God,
Alone.
Alone with my problems and my sorrows,
Alone with my decisions,
Alone with my responsibilities,
Alone with my hopes.
Alone.

Except—
Except for a friend who promised to pray for me,
Except for family and dear ones, past and present,
    who lend me their strength,
Except for Jesus who lived and died for me,
Except for the community that Jesus called his own body.

Here I stand, O God,
Not alone.
Here I stand
Surrounded by this great Cloud of Witnesses.

Here we stand.
Thank you, Gracious God.
Thank you.

Myra Nagel, in *The Inviting Word Adult Leader's Guide*, Year One
(Cleveland, Ohio: United Church Press, 1994). © 1994 by United
Church Press. Used by permission.

All That Is Within Me—Bless God

Bless God, O my soul, and all that is within me, bless God's holy name. God is merciful and gracious, slow to anger and abounding in steadfast love.

Psalm 103:1, 8

Bible Reading:	Psalm 103
Additional Bible Readings:	Jeremiah 1:4–10
	or Isaiah 58:9b–14
	Psalm 71:1–6
	Hebrews 12:18–29
	Luke 13:10–17

Enter the Word

- What does it mean to you to "bless God"?
- What are your greatest blessings? How have you praised God for them?

Begin by reading "Bless God, O My Soul," found on page 237. Consider ways in which the words to this song remind you of God's bountiful blessings in your own life.

Now read Luke 13:10–13 from one of today's additional readings. Close your eyes and replay this healing act in your imagination. The woman responds to her healing by praising God. Perhaps she jumped up and down, as if dancing for joy in her straight, freed body. Imagine Jesus' reaction to the woman's joy as he watched her praise God.

Now read Psalm 103. Close your eyes and remember the words

you just read. Perhaps one portion of the psalm especially spoke to you. You may have remembered an occasion like that of the woman described in Luke 13, a time of thanksgiving and praise. Reflect on your memory for a few moments. Bow your head in prayer. If you are able, stand up, stretch, and reach to God as a gesture of praise.

Reread the psalm and count the number of times "mercy" and "love" are mentioned. This psalmist experienced healing through the love of God. Try to remember and relive a time when you felt healed, renewed, forgiven, and loved. Praise God for this experience, perhaps by reading aloud "Bless God, O My Soul."

Conclude your study by reading Jeremiah 1:4–10, Isaiah 58:9b–14, Psalm 71:1–6, and Hebrews 12:18–29. Look for ways in which these passages show forth God's blessings.

> *I praise you that your love, mercy, and forgiveness have blessed me, Compassionate God. Amen.*

Engage the Word

- How might God's people respond to the blessing—the "good word"—about which the psalmist sings?

The psalms often are, or include, prayers addressing God. However, today's reading from Psalm 103 begins with the words "Bless God, O my soul." Yet it does not end there.

The psalm ends by calling to God's angels, mighty ones, hosts, ministers, and all God's works to bless God (Psalm 103:20–22). An individual's blessing of God with "all that is within me" (v. 1) belongs in the context of "everything that breathes" (Psalm 150:6) blessing and praising God.

Christian worship often includes a benediction, a "good word," that pronounces God's good word or blessing upon a congregation. For people to bless God means to respond to the God who already has blessed them, to say a good word to God and bless God's holy name (v. 1).

To speak of God's holy name is to speak of God's nature. God is holy and whole with full integrity. This holy God is a healing God who wants for all life to be made whole. The psalmist blesses God for all God's benefits ("good deeds") that make life whole (v. 2).

In verses 3–5 the psalmist continues to speak to the psalmist's own soul or self about what this holy God does. God forgives iniquity, heals diseases, redeems from destruction, crowns with love and mercy, satisfies with good, and renews life. In each instance the psalmist speaks very personally with the use of "you" and "your."

But in verses 6–7 the psalmist shifts from second person address to third person proclamation, from the more intimate and personal to the more public and social. These verses proclaim that God works for vindication and justice for the oppressed (v. 6). They point to Moses' and God's liberating deeds for Israel (v. 7). The Bible maintains a balanced combination of both God's personal and public healing action.

Psalm 103:8 tells of God's nature: "merciful and gracious, slow to anger and abounding in steadfast love." Mercy, grace, and love correspond with God's holy, whole-making, healing nature.

Verses 10–13 are among the most moving parts of Psalm 103. God's mercy and grace and love mean that God "does not deal with us according to our sins, nor repay us according to our iniquities" (v. 10). If God did, all would be lost. No, instead the magnitude of God's love is as high as the heavens (v. 11), and God's removal of wrongs from people is as far as the east is from the west (v. 12). God's compassion is the compassion of a father for his children (v. 13).

Verses 14–18 contrast the mortality and transience of human life with that steadfast love of God that is "from everlasting to everlasting" (v. 17) for those who respond to and bless God.

Respond to the Word

- How might you help someone else identify God's blessings and offer praise for them?
- What blessings will you praise God for today?

Go with the Word

Bless God, O My Soul

(Response)
Bless God, O my soul!
All within me bless God's name!
Bless God, who was, and is,
and shall ever be the same!

When we suffer, God sends healing;
when we sin, our God forgives;
From the grave our God redeems us,
and by grace, we rise to live!

With compassion God works justice
when oppression shackles truth;
Like the phoenix, God restores us
to the vigor of our youth.

God will not be always chiding,
nor forever angry be;
God will deal with us in mercy,
not according to our sin.

As a parent's love is endless,
so God's mercy follows us;
For the One who framed our being
well recalls that we are dust!

God removes all our transgressions
far as east is from the west;
For the grace of God is great as
heaven stands high above the earth!

"Bless God, O My Soul" (Psalm 103), words by Russell E. Sonafrank II,
1988, rev. 1993, words copyright © 1987 by Hope Publishing Co.,
Carol Stream IL 60188. All rights reserved. Used by permission.

Index of Scriptures

Hebrew Scriptures

Gospels

Epistles and Other New Testament Scriptures

Apocryphal/Deuterocanonical Books